A Cry for Tomorrow 76859 ...

A Cry
for Tomorrow
76859 ...

Berry Nahmia

Translated from the Modern Greek
by David R. Weinberg

Sephardi and Greek Holocaust Library
Volume IV

WIPF & STOCK · Eugene, Oregon

Wipf and Stock Publishers
199 W 8th Ave, Suite 3
Eugene, OR 97401

A Cry For Tomorrow 76859 ...
By Nahmia, Berry and Weinberg, David R
Copyright © 2011 by Weinberg, David R., All rights reserved.
Softcover ISBN-13: 978-1-7252-7242-2
Hardcover ISBN-13: 978-1-7252-7241-5
eBook ISBN-13: 978-1-7252-7243-9
Publication date 3/16/2020
Previously published by Bloch Publishing, 2011

Dedication

I wrote this book in memory of all my people whom I loved and lost in the crematoria of Auschwitz.

I dedicate it, however, to my beloved children, Viko and Rita, and her husband Seefi, who through their love, encouraged me to write it one day because they wanted to learn all the details of my horror during the Second World War.

Also, I dedicate this book to my beloved grandchildren, Bianca and Berry, and my beloved great-grandchildren, Eitan, Daniel, Benyo, and Tamar, who I am sure, with deep feeling and great devotion will relate it to their children who, in turn, will relate it to the generations to come.

I wish for it to remain as a memorial to my beloved husband, Mendes, who gave me such a beautiful family that is for me the meaning of my survival.

Special thanks to my dear niece, philologist-historian Odet Varon, who with much love and devotion edited my entire text.

I thank as well, all my friends, men and women, especially those companions of my prison days who survived and assisted me with dates and details of the various events we lived through together during that same period.

♦ ♦ ♦

I especially thank David Weinberg for this English translation. He succeeded in giving life to my every thought and even translated the most subtle of my feelings. His translation is indeed worthy and close to perfection.

Translator's Note

I was introduced to Berry Nahmia in the Athens synagogue at a holiday reception. She showed me the numbers on her arm. I slowly caressed them with my hand and then embraced her. We became friends. Sometime later, she gave me a signed copy of her book published in Greek. It was then that I told her I would translate it into English as a gesture of friendship and as a contribution to Holocaust studies. I hope I have caught most every nuance of her thought and emotion.

Since then, as I have come to know Berry not only as a survivor, but also as an individual. My admiration for her has soared. Her achievement is not only her incredible survival and then the writing of this book. Her achievement is her acquired wisdom and her tempered soul, which has purged itself of hate. How miraculous!

I am very grateful to my Assistant, Nancy Hauri, for editing and shepherding this translation toward publication.

David R. Weinberg

♦♦♦

This translation for Nadia

Song of Songs

How lovely is my love
in her everyday dress
with a little comb in her hair.
Girls of Auschwitz
girls of Dachau
have you seen the one I love?

We saw her on the long journey.
She wasn't wearing her everyday dress
or the little comb in her hair.

How lovely is my love
caressed by her mother
kissed by her brother.
No one knew how lovely she was.
Girls of Belsen
girls of Mauthausen
have you seen the one I love?

We saw her in the frozen square
with a number on her white arm
and a yellow star over her heart.

The quotations appearing here from my *Song* are not given as a "permission," but as an ever so slight offering to the tragic experience which the writer of this book herself represents.

Iacovos Kambanellis

INTRODUCTION TO THE SERIES

This is the fourth volume to be published in The Sephardi and Greek Holocaust Library series, whose purpose it is to fill a serious lacuna in the sad tale of the Holocaust. There is a dearth of publications on the Sephardi and Greek experiences both in terms of memoirs and scholarly studies of the period. True, there is an increasing number of publications in Greek, Hebrew, Spanish, and French; however, this material has not been submitted to the searching analysis that characterizes similar materials dealing with the variety of Ashkenazi experiences during the tragic decades of the 1930s and 1940s. The studies to be offered in this series will present to both scholars and the general public a range of materials heretofore not available in English so that the story of other communities devastated by the Nazis, marginalized for a variety of reasons by scholarly research, may find their place in the broader narrative as well as provide for their descendants an answer to the question: What happened to our relatives and ancestors in the war years?

This series comprises two categories of materials:

I. Documents, reports, memoirs which are contemporary to the events of the period. The first volume of the series includes seminal materials in this category. Later volumes contain more recently written memoirs that add new dimensions to the experience of the Sephardi and Greek Jews.

II. Scholarly studies on the Sephardi and Greek Holocaust.

On behalf of the editorial committee, we wish to express our gratitude to Sephardic House under whose auspices this series is being published. Support for this series has been graciously given by The Conference on Jewish Material Claims Against Germany, The Memorial Foundation for Jewish Culture, the Lucius M. Littauer Foundation, The Recanati Foundation in memory of Raphael Recanati, and private donors Dianne Cadesky in memory of Esther Tivoli and Molly Edell, and Victor Besso.

Steven Bowman
Series editor
Cincinnati, 2010

Contents

Preface . . . . **xiii**

1
First Years in Kastoria **3**
   My Kastoria, My religious heritage, Early memories,
Other memories, My adolescence, School days, October 28, 1940,
Italian occupation

2
Under the Yoke **11**
   Walls, Dora, The hour has come, The Jews of Thessaloniki,
The Star of David, Counting their lights

3
The Ghettos **21**
   Eviction, My high school as ghetto, Leaving Kastoria,
Harmankió ghetto, Still in Harmankió

4
The Road to Auschwitz **33**
   In the trains

5
Auschwitz **39**
   Auschwitz Station, Auschwitz, Marching to music, *Selektion*,
Block 10 — Dr. Mengele, The "Hospital",
Diary of the Auschwitz midwife, Block 11, The crematoria,
Testimonies by Greek *Sonderkommandos* Danny Bennahmias and
Marcel Nadjari, Malla did not escape, *Aussenkommando*,
Kanadakommando, They exterminated the Gypsies,
Working in Kanada, Stressful moments, Control upon control,
Soulless diamonds, The dangerous trick, Life and death scenarios,
The "premium", Brezinka, A voice from *Sonderkommando*,
Forty braidings a day, My hands, The alarm clock of the German guard,
Warning from *Sonderkommando*, The revolt betrayed,
The crematoria blown up, January 18 — evacuation of Auschwitz

6
The Death March 123
Pawns of the Third Reich, Ravensbruck, Retsov, Human nature

7
Toward Freedom 153
   May 1, 1945, Liberation by the Russians, Typhus, Lice,
   The waltz contest, The flirt, The road of return, In the train,
   My cousin again, Berlin, Our Greek group, Decampment of
   the Greeks, Brussels, A marriage proposal , An adoption
   proposal, Repatriation

Postscript 181

Glossary 185

Appendix 187

Preface

Today at last, I begin my important book.... As I go along writing it, I don't know what course it will take. I do know one thing, that the goal I have set, which has occupied my mind these many years, remains unswerving: to write something for posterity that relates the full experience of my life acquired unwillingly and under the violence of other fellowmen.

It is not at all easy to dredge up situations and experiences that the mind chases away, which memory refuses to relive. Moreover, even at this moment as I prepare to begin, I feel internal strife, a conflict, a division, where one side threatens the other.

One voice tells me: Don't return to the past, to the war, to the barbarism, to the hell, to the darkness. Don't scratch a wound that is ready to hemorrhage. It will be painful! It is best to forget, because you won't be able to withstand living through it all over again.

The other voice: No, for God's sake, don't bury, don't suppress these ghosts, these demons deep inside you, because they will always remain dormant, and only die with you. You will drag them along forever like an affliction. They will eat away at your entrails until little by little you are entirely devoured. Bring them to the surface. Do it first for your own benefit, for your own sake ... perhaps you will feel relieved and renewed. And what's more, you have a duty to future generations. They must know and remember that what happened must never be forgotten, so that it never happens again!

Thirty-eight years have passed since the Holocaust of six million Jews, and I still have not been able to speak or write about it, except once, when I told my husband everything. Then I closed myself up again, concealed it, covered it over, hoping that the passage of time would bring me forgetfulness and peace.

But I was unable to find peace, for the nightmare I feared confronting, feared looking at straight in the eye — tortured me. I constantly fought with myself, sometimes playing the role of victim, sometimes that of defense counsel, and sometimes that of judge. Dreadful! For many of us who came back, survival was and is more difficult than the Holocaust itself.

And while I go on, agonizing thus the whole life long with the same familiar demons, I suddenly discover that I have grown up, matured. I am full of experience, wisdom, knowledge — all abstracted

A Cry for Tomorrow 76859 ...

from the great book of my life, which I lived so intensely.

And I ask myself whether today, now, the hour, the right moment has come to dredge up everything inside me for all to see, hoping it will perhaps carry a message of Peace, Love, and Fraternity to the present world and the generations to come.

November 7, 1985

* * * * *

Among responses to Berry Nahmia's "great book of my life" was the following:

December 5, 1996

Dear, dear Betty [sic],

Of course I remember our meetings...

I read your book and was deeply moved by its pain as much as by its message. Yours is an important testimony.

With all my good wishes –

Elie Wiesel

A Cry for Tomorrow 76859 ...

First Years in Kastoria

My Kastoria

My heart and soul journey to a Byzantine town of Macedonia shaped like a small peninsula and bathed by the tranquil waters of a beautiful lake. My Kastoria. There I find myself a small, carefree little girl in the narrow lanes of my neighborhood where housewives sitting on stone steps whisper to each other ... I see myself in my paternal home at my window, gazing at the mountain in the distance, at the mill opposite, at the typical two-oared boats, at the fishermen with their nets!

In my mind's eye, I watch the day dawn as the sun rises and shines brightly on the freshly whitewashed houses and their courtyards. I see the Byzantine churches, the bell tower, and the entire castle! I even see the enchanting approach of evening! Over there is the moon. I see it, majestic and golden, glowing from the top of the mountain with its reflection in the lake like a red sphere thrown from high above!

My God, how I yearn to clasp all this beloved beauty tightly in my arms, to become one with it — myself with the place I was born, grew up, and loved.

I want to bring my childhood world back to life — grandfather and grandmother, my father and my mother, brothers and sisters, cousins and friends, with their boundless love, kindness, discipline, and old values. Yes, even their "you must nots" and all the things that at the time were so meaningful and beautiful!

My religious heritage

Race and religion are inherited by chance. I could have been born Muslim somewhere else, or Christian Orthodox, or anything else — as if by lottery. Lo and behold, from the day you are born you feel a label placed on you by your parents, because their parents attached the same to them. My label read: "You are a Jew." It weighed rather heavily on me. I remember many "musts" on my shoulders as I grew older.

A Cry for Tomorrow 76859 ...

I was brought up according to the moral principles of Moses' "Ten Commandments" and had to adhere to them faithfully. "Love," they say, and "Honor your father and mother." "Do not steal." I had to learn the history of my ancestors from generation to generation — of Abraham, Isaac, and Jacob. I studied the teachings and philosophy of monotheism.

We ate only kosher meat, thought to be healthier by our religion. We celebrated the feast days with different meanings than those of our Christian friends. Passover, for example, which occurs at about the same time as Christian Easter, was for us a remembrance of the exodus of the Jewish people from Egypt.

I later learned about religious antagonism, the persecutions of my race, the pogroms, the wars, the heroism and struggles of the Diaspora. And finally, I learned of the expulsion of the Jews from Spain in 1492, when, hunted and homeless, they arrived on the coasts of Italy and the Adriatic, on the mountains and the plains of the interior. They settled in Kastoria, Thessaloniki, and Monasteri-Bitolia with their own manners and customs, their ways of thinking, and most of all their language. It then became clear to me why grandfather and grandmother spoke to me in Spanish and quite naturally conveyed this language and its idioms to us.

From all this, I later became aware of the richness of the family tradition I had inherited, of the depth of my roots and my origins, of the shape of my life. My very being was prepared to take its place in this established society and to develop and function within it.

Early memories

In Martin Gray's *Book of Life** I read:

> Childhood is a spring of water that irrigates the man to come. It can drown him.
> With this water of origin, man can make his way through life.
> He can quench his thirst or poison himself with it.
> One must be careful with childhood.

It is true that one cannot deny or erase childhood memories. They are forever etched inside as a personal history. That which is

---

*Martin Gray, *A Book of Life to Find Happiness, Courage, and Hope*, New York, 1975, p. 39.

First Years in Kastoria

remembered remains throughout the journey of one's life.

At this moment, I'm not sure at what point my childhood memories begin. I wonder when one begins to remember oneself. Which is the first memory? Is it perhaps the one that lies buried inside and holds on forever, or the one most vivid, that comes easily and is expressed as if being lived again?

At this moment I feel the need to return far into the past and stop somewhere ... to the time I was a four or five year old child. I see myself very tiny. One day all the grown-ups in my house were crying! Strangely, everyone was caressing and hugging me. Why? In order to finally tell me, very haltingly, in words I didn't fully understand — that my mother had died. I can't describe how I felt at the time. One thing my little mind did grasp at that moment was that something terrible had happened.

I asked over and over, "Why won't I see my mother again?" It was beyond my comprehension. And the more they explained to me, the more I told myself that it isn't possible for God, that sweet, merciful God, to take her to heaven with Him. No, I said, He's not at all good to me.

I wanted my mama, I needed her every moment, and she loved me very much. Why did she leave? It was unfair, that's how I felt ... I was in pain, a lot of pain. I remember it as the first terrible pain of my most tender age. It was the first blow that scarred my sensitive little soul and changed my life.

Other memories
Every day it seems I heard a certain song, an internal voice, arising warm and strong within me — shaping me, raising me, nourishing and strengthening my body and soul. I was becoming a tall, dark, slim, pretty girl, they told me. An uncle of mine, who liked me very much, called me *"Mignonne"* and I loved hearing it.

My house, though large, sometimes seemed small to me. I felt confined. That's why, I recall, I would run and glue myself to my open window and stare at the horizon, waiting like a bird to grow up, to sprout wings, and fly swiftly outside on my own.

Grandfather and grandmother loved me dearly, and they also loved my brother who was three years younger. Later, four other children arrived, one after another, by my stepmother. I loved them very much and still feel that way today.

It was a blessing growing up in a house full of children in

accordance with our traditions. The habits and rules in the house were those of grandfather and grandmother with their patriarchal views about the family, the household, and honor.

My father was very youthful, and for his time had a modern outlook. He was a hardworking honest merchant who possessed a very mature social awareness. I had a special love for him and I admired his wisdom, his intelligence, and his energy. I always liked to be near him, to accompany him everywhere as I was growing up. Besides, I was his pride and joy. I felt it, and he showed it without speaking about it!

Remembering myself as a child at that time, I see a sensitive little girl, pampered, but polite, who nevertheless had a hidden flame inside her and watched for the appropriate opportunity.

My adolescence

What strong emotion I feel when I bring back memories of the first awakenings of my adolescence! It is at that time you discover your strength, like birds wanting to fly on their own, or like flower buds readying to blossom. Human spring! You gaze at the world for the first time and run toward it with optimism. You set goals, you dream, and hope your dreams come true beyond measure.

Everything seemed wonderful to me then and I slowly acquired self-confidence, belief in people, my first friendships, and those first throbs of love. I enjoyed everything in my environment, especially the way I grew up and lived among a mix of Jewish-Christian manners, customs, and local traditions in my Kastoria! It was then, I recall, that I learned to dance, laugh, and sing.

I can't say what my greater joy was when I see myself back in Kastoria at that age. Was it the walks with my girl friends to St. Thanasis church in summer? Or was it when we went to the pier with the boys close by, teasing us? Or again, was it in the middle of winter when we were wrapped in our warm, heavy coats, woolen gloves, doubled-tied scarves around our head and neck, and rubber boots on our feet? Or truly, was it when we would go sliding on the frozen lake with pointed wooden sticks?

Sometimes the temperature would fall to eleven degrees below zero and it was bitter cold. That's when Kastoria was covered with snow and the lake frozen for months. We would go outside for snowball fights. But the slopes were our greatest fun. They were our "slides." We children, I recall, didn't walk on the icy snow, we just kept sliding — falling down and getting up, and again, falling down and standing up. What an unforgettable time!

We lived peacefully and harmoniously with our Christian neighbors, both in our social relations and in our jobs, because there was mutual respect, friendship, and love.

I remember that each year on January 6th, the Day of Epiphany, the custom was to visit our friend, Theano Kovatsi, to wish her a happy name day which she always celebrated. Her parents and sisters Ritsa, Meni, and Louda, always received us with great joy. And then there would follow such a wonderful party — girlfriends merrymaking until late at night! On January 7th and 8th, just before St. John's Day, I remember, there was a carnival, the *Pateritsa,* and we would rush to Dultso Square to see it — a traditional Christian festival called *Ragoutsiaria*. All Kastoria stood there to celebrate. Children and grown-ups in masquerade danced in the streets to the accompaniment of popular musical instruments.

These Christmas holidays seemed endless because the preparations started a month earlier. We children, being on vacation, were carefree and enjoying ourselves right up to the night before school, when we would fall exhausted into bed only to wake up the following morning to go back to our daily routine.

School days

Jewish education was obligatory for me, but only through primary school. During that time we studied both Greek and Hebrew. In those first six years, I studied many things including *The Old Testament*. I even learned to speak Hebrew fluently, the language of my religious ancestors. But when I entered high school, I completely abandoned my Hebrew. I changed, or rather I acquired more ancestors. Why not? This time our ancient ancestors were Socrates, Plato, Sophocles, Thucydides, and Homer.

There were only a few Jewish girls in the high school. We were called "the bouquet of flowers" by our new teachers and by all the people of Kastoria without exception, because they liked us.

We excelled in school events. I remember the parades, especially the one in celebration of St. Minas, November 11th, the day when Kastoria was liberated from the Turks. We marched in the first row, and were even the flag-bearers. They were proud of us and we were proud of ourselves!

In this state of happiness, of youthful enthusiasm, precisely when

A Cry for Tomorrow 76859 ...

one has thirst for life — war found me, the Second World War.

October 28, 1940

Early, very early in the morning, the bells started ringing loudly! Alarm! Everyone was shouting: "General mobilization! Metaxas said 'NO' to the Italians!"

I was taken completely by surprise by it all and couldn't grasp the reality. From that moment on, where would these events eventually lead me? I had heard people tell war stories, but those things happened only in narratives, in books that belonged to the past, to the years of our grandfathers. They couldn't happen now, during my life.

Could it be only some small incident that would end soon? That's what I wanted to believe. But the airplanes over our heads were not joking, they were dropping bombs!

Soldiers — our boys — were leaving for the front lines. Young men, even brothers of my dad and mom, were fighting the Italians in Albania, and fighting courageously, the poor kids! Uproar! Shouting! Danger all around!

War! War! "Let's take the children, the old folks, and go to the villages," my father said, "perhaps we'll save ourselves from the bombs."

Crowded together for days in my older uncle's cellar, the entire family and all our neighbors hid until the air raids stopped.

November 1st, November 3rd, still continuous bombing. Truly, how did we all come out of there alive? In reality Kastoria suffered very few victims at the time, I recall, as if the Italians deliberately missed the city, for the bombs dropped into the lake.

At dusk, just before nightfall on the evening of November 3rd, in order to escape the bombings, dad, having gathered us together, courageously guided us through the fields to a mountain village with the help of his white horse, the beautiful white horse we loved so much. (There were no cars then.)

In the village, we would spend the day outside in trenches. At night, we rested in a little rented house. This went on every day for three or four months. Running for cover! Anxiety! Bombs! But our soldiers successfully repelled the danger. They entered Albania, reached Elbasan ... Korytsa.

Patriotic songs were composed which were sung throughout Greece! Sofia Vembo, the heroic singer of 1940, went to the front lines to encourage our soldiers with her warm voice, singing:

First Years in Kastoria

> Sons, sons of Greece,
> fighting fiercely
> on the mountains.
> Sons, we all pray
> to the sweet Virgin,
> for your return ...

I remember singing too, sometimes loudly with enthusiasm, sometimes secretly to myself in prayer with my eyes turned toward heaven ... begging for the safe return of our relatives, friends, and all our Greek young men — our lads.

Suddenly everything changed. Events now followed one another unexpectedly at an accelerated pace, creating confusion and concern all over Greece. The enthusiasm and pride we felt for our fighting men was not to last. Germany invaded Greece. German boots swept up all of Macedonia very rapidly.

I remember the shocking, black day when *stukas,* German warplanes, screaming through the sky, unleashed bombs all around like rain. We couldn't breathe! And even more shocking was the terror later when enemy soldiers entered the villages and cities, making them tremble like an earthquake.

It was April 14, 1941 when we finally realized we were caught like rats in a trap. All at once we found ourselves at their mercy, encircled by wild beasts, hearing the names — "GERMANS," "NAZIS," "SS"!

Italian occupation

The Germans divided Greece in two: They gave Athens and Kastoria to their Italian collaborators, while Thessaloniki was kept completely in the hands of the Germans. Thus, approximately 60,000 Jews, now German prisoners of occupied Thessaloniki were cut off from us, many of whom were our relatives. Rarely and only secretly did we hear news from them.

The Italian occupation of Kastoria was bearable. The Italians, a Mediterranean people, behaved humanely toward us all. Moreover, the soldiers themselves confessed that they did not want the war, and they proved it. So during that period, our lives took a peculiar turn — a life under occupation, but bloodless. It was a time when everyone tried in every way possible to survive the great hunger of 1941, '42 and '43.

Schools reopened. I returned to my high school class, to finish and eventually receive my diploma. At the same time, I took private French lessons. I remember my teacher being paid one kilo of flour for each lesson.

Despite everything, these memories would remain the last glimmer of family life for me. I was still in my world then, among my many relatives, among my childhood girlfriends and boyfriends, among the people of my faith in that beautiful world of mine — a Jewish community of 1000 persons who lived lovingly together.

And moreover, I was still in school.

Under the Yoke

Walls

With no consideration, no pity, no shame,
They've built walls around me, thick and high.
And now I sit here feeling hopeless.
I can't think of anything else: this fate gnaws my mind-
because I had so much to do outside.
When they were building the walls, how could I not have noticed!
But I never heard the builders, not a sound.
Imperceptibly they've closed me off from the outside world.

C.P. Cavafy*

One day, I recall, shortly before I received my high school diploma, my principal, Mr. Delaportas, went to my dad's shop to speak with him about me. I learned of it the following day when in my presence, grandfather asked my father, "What was Berry's teacher telling you for so long? Isn't she good in school?"

"On the contrary," Dad replied. "He told me that since she's about to finish high school, she should go to Athens to study drama, because she has rare talent. He said it would be a pity not to."

Grandfather became furious as soon as he understood. I remember he began trembling all over and shouting: "In our family, we don't produce actors! Be careful with her, it will bring great shame on us!"

Poor grandpa, even if I had wanted to, I couldn't have done it. The Germans had us in a trap. They were the ones issuing orders to the Italians. I had no right to venture beyond the city limits anymore. How could I have left? I was a Jew, and all Jews were under surveillance.

I didn't want to believe that because of our religion, we were

---

*From *C.P. Cavafy, Collected Poems* trans. by Edmund Keeley and Philip Sherrard. New Jersey, 1983.

already suffering the first arbitrary violations of our human freedom, of our lives. I realized I didn't even have the slightest right to think of my studies. Suddenly I felt huge high walls surrounding me, barring me from the rest of the world — just like the walls in Cavafy's poem.

Dora

One evening on a "name day," I went to visit a distant aunt of mine. At her house, I met two young men, foreigners who were acquaintances of my aunt. They were two brothers, twenty and twenty-five years old. The twenty-year old had an ordinary face and looked typical for his age, let's say nothing special. The twenty-five year old was something else — a rare male beauty, reminding one of those handsome, heroic movie stars. He was a tall, dark, good-looking fellow with incredible light blue eyes and black hair. I remember staring at him, dazzled.

Both were exhausted, however, and said they had come a long distance on foot from a Serbian monastery in order to escape the Germans.

"But why?" I asked. "What are the Germans doing to Jews?"

"They seize our property, our houses, and deport us to concentration camps somewhere far away. All our relatives have been arrested. We saw them with our own eyes as they were being taken away. We managed to hide, and after a great deal of suffering, escaped and arrived here in Kastoria."

The next day and the day after, more of them arrived in the same way, two by two, until there were about twenty of them. Later, four or five more families came from Belgrade. These unfortunate people ran to the Italian command post, seeking asylum. The Italians again behaved humanely, and with great compassion allowed them to stay in Kastoria, which was under their occupation.

In a short period of time, all these young newcomers from Yugoslavia became an integral part of our company, and in that time of occupation, were a source of joy, a new wave, that somehow eased and warmed our uncertain and disturbed lives. These Yugoslavian Jews found in us a measure of comfort too, a new family. Unfortunately, this was the reason they stayed with us and why most of them did not leave. Because of this, they eventually shared our same fate and destiny to the bitter end.

In this group of Yugoslavian youth there were only two girls. One was called Dora, who later became my friend and played an important role in all my subsequent life. Dora looked older than I, and what attracted me to her was the way she reasoned. In my eyes she was very strong and down-to-earth. She knew how to confront difficult situations and I admired her knowledge and experience.

She had hidden in the attic of her home for days, she said, so as not to give herself up to the Germans. Having convinced her older, but very cowardly brother to join her, they disguised themselves as elderly peasants and practically tumbled their way down the Yugoslavian border to Greece.

Simply listening to her, just being with her, I felt like an ignorant and inexperienced child whose head was still in the clouds. I admired her strength and determination, and remember very much wanting to become like her.

"Are you ready now, my dear Berry, to face the Germans as a Jew?" she asked me one day.

"But why, dear Dora? What have I done to the Germans to single me out just for being a Jew?"

"Are you ready to cope with brutality, hunger, beatings, humiliation?"

"But ... for heaven sake!"

"I want you to know just one thing," she went on. "A person can survive without food for forty days provided he gets water and above all — note this — provided his morale stays high. Bear that in mind, Berry dear, only if one's morale remains high."

"But how — how can morale stay high? It takes enormous strength. If one doesn't eat, where does the strength come from to endure?" (Being inexperienced, that's how I reasoned at the time.)

"I have read many books," she said, "and learned from them. I've met people who told me how they suffered hell on earth because of their ideology, but with superhuman strength, survived — without hands, without nails, without food — because they wanted to live."

"But Dora, are you referring to the Middle Ages? This is the Twentieth Century. These things don't happen anymore, it's inhuman."

I listened to her carefully for hours, however, and was carried away by her convincing manner. When Dora was speaking, you had the impression you were listening to her read a stirring, fascinating book. I thought to myself ... if ever, God forbid, I find myself in a difficult situation, I must have her close by me, to absorb strength in order to survive. Otherwise I'll be lost!

A Cry for Tomorrow 76859 ...

Life went on, sometimes philosophizing with Dora, sometimes organizing informal parties for our Greek and Yugoslavian friends, our *après-midi,* which would last from early in the afternoon until just before dark.

Female company consisted of my close friends Lena Eliaou, Rebecca Pissirilou, my cousin Rebecca Zacharia, Stella Eliaou, and Paula Cohen. Together we formed an inseparable group of six.

I remember one day, just for fun, the six of us set an appointment to meet in Kastoria on May 4th, 1945, by all means — that is to say, a year and a half from then. It was a clear indication that we had a presentiment of danger, because of the anxiety from what was happening around us. Deep inside we all wished to be together on some such day, safe and sound, in the town of our birth.

I could write endless pages about these girlfriends of mine. All my childhood and adolescent years were bound up with them in common joys, emotions, agonies, and fears — all the feelings that develop real and unforgettable bonds.

I will never forget the fear and agony I went through one day because of our thoughtlessness at the time. My friend Rebecca Pissirilou once said, "You're aware the upper floor of our house is rented by Tenente Ravalli? And know what? He is never home this hour of the day, and he often disappears from Kastoria for days. I found a second key to his apartment that my father had. Let's go secretly and see what he keeps up there."

Influenced as always by Rebecca's novel ideas, I replied: "Are you sure there's no danger if we go?"

"No," she said, "don't be scared."

The word became deed. As we climbed the inner stairs of Rebecca's house and very timidly opened the door... we suddenly saw a military uniform hanging like a scarecrow in a vineyard against the wall of his hallway.

For a moment, I thought somebody was hanging there in uniform! I panicked! I couldn't move forward or backward. I don't remember how we descended the stairs and found ourselves outside again. Breathlessly, I said to my friend, "Look, from now on I'm not going to let you talk me into doing these crazy things. I was very frightened and I'm still shaking ... imagine if Ravalli was inside!"

We never told a soul, not even our other friends. We kept it a secret between us. Rebecca immediately hid the key where she found it and we never mentioned it again. But had we been clever enough at the time, and known how to search, we would have found important things: documents containing war secrets and planned actions this Tenente Pietro-Giovani Ravalli* had hidden in that upstairs Jewish apartment.

During that period, two joyful events suddenly changed the composition of our group. My cousin Rebecca with whom I was very close, was about to be married. Though still quite young, my uncle was anxious to get her settled. And my closest friend, Rebecca Pissirilou with whom I was inseparable, was getting married to Leon Franko — that tall Yugoslavian with the incredible light blue eyes and black hair I had initially met at my aunt's house. Both girls were slightly older than I.

But their marriages were their misfortune, because later things became very difficult and marriage was the reason these poor souls did not survive. Moreover, having had children right away did not help.

The hour has come

When I recall this critical time of my life, I tell myself that right now "the hour has come," the hour I have avoided confronting for years as if it were death itself.

Strangely enough I feel strong now, and as I said at the beginning, my purpose urges me on. And thus, with body and soul always inseparable, my pen is ready and willing to record all the images and details I will solemnly dredge up one after another from the depth of my subconscious. I am determined — this time willingly — to live that hell again from beginning to end.

The Jews of Thessaloniki

The Jews of Thessaloniki, who were under German occupation, suffered terribly in 1942-1943. They were obliged to wear the Jewish star on their chest so as to be set apart from others. They were imprisoned on trumped up charges. Their houses were confiscated; their possessions seized; and they were sent away to hard labor, allegedly to rebuild railway tracks, etc.

For a while, they were able to stave off forced labor by paying ransom money. But slowly and steadily, the diabolic system of the

---

*Tenente Pietro-Giovani Ravalli, an Italian lieutenant, was the most famous army officer in Kastoria at the time. Despite the fact that he was only a lieutenant, he played a very important role during the occupation.

A Cry for Tomorrow 76859 ...

Third Reich was put into place toward the "Final Solution" — the extermination and annihilation of the Jews.

In February 1943, Adolph Eichmann arrived in Thessaloniki to personally take charge of Jewish matters. In collaboration with Maximilian Merten, military counsel at the time, they laid their satanic plans for the deportation of the Jews.

Eichmann, in order to avoid resistance from the multitudes, intentionally spread the rumor that Jews transported to Cracow (Poland) with their entire families would be warmly welcomed by people of the same religion. Everyone would live there together.

We learned this news about the Jews of Thessaloniki from our Christian friends who could travel freely between Kastoria and Thessaloniki and often did so. The deportations had already begun, they said. Before leaving, people exchanged their drachmas for Polish *zlotys*. Trains full of Jews were leaving for an unknown destination and these hapless people had no idea what was in store for them.

These same German executioners didn't delay laying their plans and putting the destructive mechanisms in motion for us as well, the Jews of Kastoria. Letters sent from Poland, supposedly from our Thessalonikian brothers, were circulated house to house. These letters were written in the Judeo-Spanish dialect.

I clearly remember a letter allegedly sent by our fellow citizen, Fortunata Eliaou. Fortunata, a Jewess from Kastoria, was caught by chance in the deportations of the Thessaloniki Jews because she had gone there to visit her married daughter. Unfortunately, she, her daughter and the entire family shared the fate of so many Jews of Thessaloniki who were sent directly to the crematoria.

The letter, however, said that they had all arrived safely in Cracow; that they had been warmly welcomed by the Jewish community; that life was good and that they were waiting for us to arrive, hopefully very soon. We shouldn't have any hesitations or fear anything it said. Everything there was wonderful.

During this period of turmoil, a middle-aged couple appeared in Kastoria. I still can almost see them with their crude manners. They said they were Polish Jews. As soon as they arrived in our city, they contacted the Jewish Center showing passports stamped with the usual *Juden*, meaning "Jews." They begged for financial help, saying they were refugees who escaped from their country.

The Jewish community helped them immediately. A basic ethic fostered in the home of everyone in Kastoria, especially in Jewish families, was hospitality for travelers and assistance to the poor. I shall never forget this very beautiful lesson that I learned at home. My grandfather, a very religious man, regularly went to the synagogue to pray to his God. Very often on his way home, he would bring some stranger with him. "He comes from far away," he would say, "we must afford him hospitality, offer him food, and a place to sleep."

Likewise, many a Friday afternoon at nightfall, so nobody could recognize me, they sent me, I recall, young as I was, to take provisions to the poor — freshly home-baked bread, coal for their fire, and other necessities. Yes, I remember how they told me to knock discreetly on the door, offer these things politely, and not reveal where they came from. Grandfather always said that our religion teaches us to help the poor, but not demonstratively, so as not to insult them. "What one hand gives, the other hand must not see, my child. That's how one should help another."

These Polish Jews, being very familiar with the Jewish religion, quickly understood our Kastorian mentality. It was not long before they started going in and out of our houses, eating, drinking, and getting on well for themselves.

The Jewish community didn't fail to offer them financial assistance, but it never satisfied them and they constantly demanded more. My uncle, Zahos Zaharias, the unmarried brother of my mother who was older than I by six years, was at that time secretary of the community. He assisted Kalef Eliaou, president of our community, so my uncle, being close to the president, was informed of them.

Sometimes he would half confide in me, telling me that: "These two Polish Jews are the nightmare of our community, and to tell you the truth, they've started annoying me with their insolence."

"Let them be, poor people. They've been chased from their homes. They're to be pitied and need our help. We should assist them as much as we can." That's what I told my uncle. He did not reply, but remained very skeptical and was irritated every time he met them.

I realize now that my uncle wisely hid something from me and didn't dare tell me anything else at the time.

The Star of David

Immediately after the capitulation of Italy on September 8th, the Germans reoccupied all the regions held by their former ally and deployed their forces throughout the country to dominate Greece in its entirety. The Italian troops in Greece disbanded but were caught and became prisoners of the Germans. Some tried to escape into the mountains held by the Greek partisans, but only a few succeeded because the fury of the Nazis broke upon them. The Nazis hunted them, arrested them, caught them like birds, and squeezed them into freight cars to take them to concentration camps.

The spectacle was so horrible, even we quaked with fear. It was the first time we saw such brutality. Despairing, we asked ourselves whether we should flee also. Would it be difficult for someone to escape? Unfortunately, the Germans were already strictly guarding the isthmus, the only narrow strip of land connecting us to the opposite side. Kastoria is a small peninsula — three sides are on the lake and the other, a little strip of land.

Upon seeing the Italians being chased in such a horrible way, my father became very alarmed. The poor man felt the heavy burden of the family on his shoulders and he was only forty-two years old. He agonized over whom he should think of first, whom he should save first — the four little children ten and under, or the old folks, my grandfather and my grandmother?

One day he took me aside and spoke to me very seriously: "Look my child, I consider you a grown-up now. I trust you very much and I am sure you will be able to survive on your own. Since you're the oldest, take your brother and go to the partisans in the mountains. It's not possible for me to leave, I have the younger ones. You two at least, or whoever of you can, should go. Don't tell me when and how — just save yourselves." I looked him in the eyes and my soul felt pity for him. He was imploring me to leave and save myself.

The following day I met my Uncle Zahos and conveyed what my father had told me. I begged him to leave with me. He was clever — gifted I believed — and had many Christian friends who would help. With him I would be safer and I trusted him.

"I will tell you tomorrow whether we can leave," he said.

The following day he told me he would not be leaving. He loved a girl who was one of my good friends and without her, freedom would be useless to him.

"Then we're not going?"

"Wait a bit," he told me. "Besides, who says we're in danger? Let's all stay together."

So we waited and black fate didn't delay rolling over us.

Day after day things got worse. On Yom Kippur, Friday October 8, 1943, the German commander called on the president of the Jewish community and ordered him to immediately bring the sum of 1000 British sovereigns in retaliation for five or six young Jews, who it was rumored, had escaped Kastoria to join the partisans. The community was to be punished and from then on, fifty hostages would be executed for the slightest violation.

A collection to raise the sum was quickly begun among the wealthy, and the order was promptly obeyed. Fear and horror reigned. Fathers of all families, as well as the president of the community, appealed to older children, imploring, even threatening them, to dare not escape to the partisans, lest by leaving they endanger the rest of the families with death. My father just looked at me without saying another word, as if telling me: "What has been said will always apply."

Nobody dared make a move anymore. Every young man was thinking of his family's fate and that of the Jewish community if he were to leave.

After a week, a new order: "Jews must wear the Star of David on the chest so Jews can be distinguished from others." Now our situation worsened. A week later, another order: "All Jews are required to turn in their gold within twenty-four hours."

The community obeyed again. Everyone rushed to deposit into the hands of the commander every golden object they had hidden in their house. This tax, this ransom, bought us a few months rest and lulled us into believing that the Germans simply wanted to lay hands on our gold, and would not implement their racist laws against us.

Fatal illusion!

Counting their lights

One afternoon I walked with my Uncle Zahos, who talked to me at length and trusted me with his inner feelings about my friend. He was very much in love, poor man, and I tried to help him.

"Why haven't you told her yet? What are you waiting for?" I asked him. "Do you want me to tell her?"

"No, I'll think of something and find the way myself."

It was almost dark when we opened the door to go in where my uncle lived. Suddenly we heard voices coming from inside and readily understood that the Polish Jews were in the house, asking the rest of the family about Zahos. They wanted him urgently, asking again and again where he was and where they could find him.

"They're looking for me again ... let's go back," Zahos said. "I'll walk you home. I want to avoid those two and don't want to meet them. Whenever I see them I think they're bringing along bad news. Anyway, tonight I don't want to see them." (Because the Polish Jews knew German, they were often interpreters between the German commander and the Jewish community.)

"As you wish," I replied. "Anyway, I can't understand why you still blame them for bad news. They're Jews too. Don't you see them wearing the distinctive star on their chest like all of us? They share the same fate, poor things!"

So, he walked me home, which was just across the street, and waited for those undesirable Polish Jews to leave and disappear. I remember very well that we did not see them again that evening, which was to be our last evening in our home. What did they want him for? Even now, I still wonder about it!

Before going to bed, I went to my favorite window and stuck my face, nose, and mouth on the glass, riveting my eyes on the road in the distance beyond the opposite shore of the lake. I saw vehicles entering our Kastoria. I counted them. I counted their lights as they advanced in the dark of night. "Many military trucks are entering the city tonight, making so much noise. What could the Germans be up to?" I recall saying to myself. "It's war, what do you expect?"

I decided it was better not think so much, and fell asleep unsuspecting.

The Ghettos

Eviction

The next morning, March 24, 1944, I woke up very rested, having slept well. I stretched for a few minutes in my warm bed, enjoying the sweetness and comfort of that morning's sun as its first rays slowly penetrated my room through my windows. Then I very gently stretched my arms, raised them high above the pillow and yawned. I felt wonderful!

What I would give to return for a while to that beautiful last awakening in my bed in my father's house, and bring back that vivid image I still hold deep in my soul!

Everything was calm, beautiful, normal. Tranquillity reigned throughout the house. I hadn't realized that my father, grandfather, and brother had left for their shop at daybreak, though they usually rushed about in the morning to leave for work, trying not to make noise, so as not to wake the children.

My grandmother and stepmother were talking quietly in the kitchen. They were always preparing something there! Feeling rested and happy, I glanced one last time around my room to enjoy the serenity of the simple, youthful room which had recently become exclusively mine. My belongings: a few books, notebooks, pencils ... and the little drawer in which I kept a small mirror and a secret little letter that I used to read and re-read, smiling.

Youth is wonderful! Everything seems beautiful to you because you feel so nice. You are strong, have no pain, and constantly want to play, run, laugh.

I lazed about a little longer planning my day in my mind. Then with one motion, in a split second, I threw off my covers, got up light as feather, warm as toast. I didn't have the time to change or make a second move when I heard screams and wailing outside. What could be happening? Our house was built in the middle of a hill. I went to look at the hill from the window in my grandmother's room and noticed huge crowds running up, running down as if being chased in the road.

A Cry for Tomorrow 76859 ...

Our gate suddenly swung open wide, and in front of me I saw my aunt, my father's eldest sister, who was about fifty years old. This aunt had practically raised me with her own children, and whenever I had fever she took me to her house until I completely recovered. I remember often feigning being sick because I liked staying with her. I loved her as my mother. An armed German SS followed her into our house, shouting, threatening us, ordering us out: *Raus, verfluchte Juden, raus!* "Out, damned Jews, out!"

"What is going on? Auntie, why are you here so early in the morning with him?" Breathless, in a barely audible voice, my aunt tried to explain to us that all the men had already been taken prisoner.

"The Jewish shops have been surrounded. Everyone will be led to the High School for Girls by the Valala house, you know, near the reservoir," she told me.

The German was yelling again like a beast: "Get ready, take whatever you can carry in your hands. All Jews clear out and go to present yourselves where all your men are waiting for you. Quickly!"

"Yes, hurry up!" explained a Greek interpreter at his side.

I escaped their notice, supposedly to get ready and took my aunt aside telling her not to be afraid, that I am by her side, and that from now on each would help the other.

My aunt secretly told me she brought my mother's jewels, which she had kept for me all these years in anticipation of my marriage.

"Take them now, carry them with you. I hand them over to you," she said. "If you wish, from your own hands, give me something to give my children, because I have nothing of my own.

This whole terrible situation made me furious. I never had so many golden jewels before, so many valuable stones, such a fortune in my hands.... Everyone had told me that I was too young for these things, and that they would become mine when I grew up. And now, in this turmoil, what in the devil happened? Had I instantly grown up? What could I do? How could I hide them?

A minute later the German came again. He sensed something was going on between my aunt and me. Without warning, he attacked me — grabbed whatever he could from my hands and went away happy, howling like an animal.

Like an automaton ... I let him take the jewels without putting up any resistance, as if they weren't mine. Besides, I didn't understand at the time how it was possible to acquire such a fortune one moment, and the very next have it disappear, and lose almost everything out of

The Ghettos

my hands. They were my mother's only heirlooms.

"Let's first go to your house," I said to my aunt.

Since we were all living in the same neighborhood, it was easy to make the rounds to any of my relatives. In my aunt's upstairs storeroom we hid two or three rings of great value. They were the only jewels the German left behind for me as he forcefully grabbed them.

My poor cousins were busy collecting whatever clothes they could for themselves, and for their brothers and father, who had been rounded up in the morning. Having been unexpectedly seized at work, they had nothing with them.

I told my eighty year old grandmother who adored me, to wait for me, that I would immediately come back to help her as well as my stepmother and my little brothers and sisters, so we could all leave together to join our men.

Before closing my aunt's house we all wept bitterly. We were abandoning a house full of years of memories of hard labor and sacrifice. I was incensed and felt like exploding. So I said to my aunt, "Watch this! To vent my rage, I'm going to break every window in your house. Whoever comes here won't find even one pane of glass."

And I broke them ... broke them ... with all my being. I entered every room. I left no window, no door. My hands were hurting, my head, my whole body. I was beside myself. My poor aunt just looked at me and cried. She said nothing. I was out of my mind with what was happening to us.

"Let's get grandmother and all the others," I said decisively, "and go together to the High School for Girls to find the men."

In the street, as I was going past my house, I remembered my friend Dora who lived through the same awful moments about a year and a half before in Yugoslavia. She had hidden in the attic of her house for days, so as not to give herself up to the Germans. That time she escaped and came all the way to Kastoria on foot, only to live through the same thing again, the same "scenario."

Where, I wondered, could Dora be right now? For sure she's hidden somewhere.... She was living some distance from me, quite a way outside our Jewish neighborhood. Many times we had discussed that if the same thing happened again, she would by all means hide and wait in her house for me to come and find her. We would rendezvous. I promised her I would never give myself up to the Germans and that we would hide together. This was our agreement.

With that thought I froze and couldn't move. Suddenly I bent over. I aged. I became a very old woman. Though I was still in control of my reasoning, which ruled, all personal feelings were gone, all selfishness. No, I was not going to save only my skin. How could I abandon all my people who needed me so much at this very moment? These were the people who raised me, protected me, were proud of me, loved me, and taught me to love. How could I leave them and go off on my own?

"Let's go." I told them firmly and unequivocally, succumbing to my terrible fate. "Let's walk on our own two feet, blindly, toward our own Calvary."

With one sack on my shoulder and a bundle in each hand, I took my grandmother, little brothers and sisters, stepmother, aunts, cousins, and neighbors — all together like a flock, each close to the other — and rushed to enter our ghetto where they ordered us to go. Like birds of prey, the Gestapo were behind us with guns at our heads.

We were leaving behind forever, our houses, our existence, a whole way of life — ours and those of our ancestors who had lived here for centuries before us. Each generation had left to the next generation its history as an inheritance.

I was leaving the house where I was born and raised. I had harmed no one. But now they were forcing me to leave and accept myself as I really was — a "Jew."

My high school as ghetto

Chased and shoved like dogs by the Germans, all of us — children, grown-ups, the elderly — went pulling one another into the mousetrap. Inside, the first concern was to search for and find one's own people.

There! My poor grandfather, more than eighty years old, doubled-over despite his tall stature ... there, my brother Alberto. There, my father!

I don't recall our feelings at the moment of meeting. I only know that it was a deep, deep emotion of raging tears, of shared embrace, with a moan of unfairness emanating from out of our chests.

I don't know why, but as soon as I saw my father I felt relieved. The burden I had taken upon my shoulders was a very heavy one for me. I couldn't bear it any longer because I was still only a little girl!

The first emotions passed as each found his relatives, friends, and neighbors. We became reunited with each other and there were strong ties between us. Each one asked the other who was missing from the community and the accounting was easy and quick.

Only six young men slipped out of the hands of the German Gestapo to reach the surrounding mountains. So did a family of eight, who by chance were at the mill outside of town. They escaped the roadblock to join the partisans. How I wished to be in their position! At that moment I rediscovered my natural independence. Suddenly I felt like breaking my bonds, getting out of there, and flying far away.

But just as I had that thought, I saw my friend Dora right in front of me, like an apparition! She was the last person I expected to see there.

"You, here? How come? You didn't hide again?"

"This time it was impossible," she replied. "They took my brother from the market with all the other men and I knew he wouldn't be able to cope without me. So I came here to meet him. He's the only relative I have left."

At that moment I very selfishly felt better. Dora was always strong and fate had brought her near to me, beside me, now when I needed her most.

Without any mattress or blanket, we laid down somewhere on the ground at night, huddled up one against the other wearing just what we happened to be dressed in from home.

In the past, this building was the High School for Girls that I attended for two or three years before it merged with the High School for Boys. But now the conditions were so different, so terrible, that they completely effaced my good old student memories.

The school was a large, three-storied building where in the past, only students' voices and songs could be heard. It had been transformed into a horrible prison where approximately one thousand innocent souls were packed, not daring to breathe a word.

The following day, standing by one of the windows that looked out on a church (St. Thanasis where we used to take our unforgettable walks), someone suddenly shouted: "Quick, come and see! Tell me if you see what I see!"

Oh God, the two Polish Jews!

They were walking in the street below, free, strolling up and down. They were laughing demonstratively with heads held high turned toward the building, as if enjoying our having been caught like mice in a trap. What an irony. No longer were they wearing our star on their chest. Unbelievable!

I immediately called my Uncle Zahos and pointed them out to him. There was no doubt about it. We all came to the same conclusion.

A Cry for Tomorrow 76859 ...

The infamous two were German agents and all of us, like simpletons, believed them and felt sorry for them. Those dastardly Germans skillfully deceived us royally by every abominable means. They had been preparing our arrest for a long time.

Horrors! Every moment we encountered a new order, a new threat: all valuables taken with us were to be surrendered. Even if someone left something in a cache in his house, he must confess to it at once.

For a moment my heart almost broke when two armed SS picked up my uncle Isaac Zaharias.

"We're going back to your house and you'll tell us where you've hidden your gold," they told him.

The poor man succumbed and followed them, trembling. He was the beloved uncle of my mother, very fond of me, and considered me an inseparable part of his family. Almost every day I would stop by his house and I often slept there with my cousins.

After hours of agony, my cousins, my aunt, and I saw when they finally brought him back completely debilitated.

In a state of agitation, everyone threw everything, even their wedding rings, into the ghetto toilet and flushed it. Thus, having stripped ourselves of even the smallest golden pin, we got rid of everything.

Soon afterward, a new shock: Our handsome young friend, Moise Russo* returned, bent over and disheartened. He was the only one who courageously dared to hide in Kastoria. It lasted only twenty-four hours. Coming very carefully out of his hiding place, he decided to ask a Christian friend, a schoolmate, to help him. His friend immediately gave him whatever he needed. But Moise, not wishing to place him in danger, did not stay at his house. He left immediately, planning to cross the opposite hill, get out of the city, and make it to the mountain. Unfortunately, even before crossing the hill, a German patrol stopped him, quickly discovered his identity, and dragged him to our ghetto to share our fate.

For two or three days to our great surprise, the German occupation authorities allowed some of our Christian friends to visit us. I will never forget that two of my classmates, Dota Krassa and Soultana Aivazi, came to see me in the ghetto during those difficult

---

*Moise suffered in the concentration camps of Poland and came back safe. He married my friend Lena Eliaou, emigrated to America where he died. They had three children and grandchildren.

The Ghettos

moments of mine. Dota brought me many things from her house, and as she was living nearby, she came again and again. Soultana, who worried about us all, asked me if I needed anything so she could bring it next time.

"Ok," I said to her, "I'll tell you. Tomorrow you can bring me a cake." That's what I remember asking her for, I don't know why ... maybe because I was beginning to feel very hungry.

"Come, I'll see you off now." I said, and took her by the arm. As we were walking and talking, we exited the block without realizing it and went past the guard. When I understood I had overstepped the allowed limits, I automatically ran back in a hurry, because for a moment, I thought the guard would shoot me in the back. Breathless from fear, I found myself inside again.

Soultana, waving farewell to me, was leaving while I stood there nailed to the spot. Unable to move, I watched her depart as she walked toward her house, free. I was in shock and couldn't pull myself together.

That evening after dark, I closed my eyes and visualized the scene of the afternoon with Soultana. Suddenly startled, I shouted to myself, "Oh God!" It was dawning on me what happened! Now that I could recall it clearly, I realized that the guard hadn't paid any attention to me at all, nor did he suspect that I was Jewish and Soultana Christian. Moreover, I wasn't wearing the star on my chest (there was no reason to). Then why was I scared? Why did I go back? Once I had already gone past the guard, why didn't I tell Soultana to take me home with her? It would have been easy for her to help me escape to the mountains and join the partisans.

I was beside myself with anger and hysterically beat my head against the wall. "You coward," I shouted to myself. How unacceptable! Tomorrow, for sure, as soon as Soultana arrives I'll ask her to take me home with her. I must get out of here, I said to myself over and over.

But the next morning, as soon as we opened our eyes, we heard a new order: "From now on, Christians will not be allowed in the Jews' ghetto."

Of course, I never saw Soultana again....

They doubled the guards and prepared the moves and procedures for transferring us to Thessaloniki as soon as possible. Shortly thereafter, shouting and threatening, they took everyone down into the street opposite.

A Cry for Tomorrow 76859 ...

Mothers with newborn babies in their arms; small children all alone crying; old men and women, paralyzed and disabled, unable to drag their feet, were pulled with rage down to the street and ordered to stand in two lines. Everyone at attention. They counted us and counted us, calculated and recalculated.... After a while, in the same awful manner, they closed us in again for one more night.

During this horrible time, my first cousin, Regina Cohen, wrote a message on the wall of our ghetto for her schoolmate, Tasitsa Valala. (She lived in the house next door to the ghetto building that the Germans had requisitioned. At the time it belonged to the Valala family.)

The message read as follows:

> My dear Tasitsa,
> When you read these words,
> I shall no longer be alive.
> I shall have withered in a foreign land.
> Shed a tear for me.
> Whether I live or die.

This is what Tasitsa herself later related to me. Tasitsa had learned Regina's message by heart and from what she told me, for years she never let her mother paint that wall, so she could see it and remember Regina, who never came back.

Leaving Kastoria

There was no more postponement. The following day they led us to the trucks bound for Thessaloniki. These were the same vehicles and trucks I myself counted the night of March 23rd, when glued to the window of my room. I had counted their lights one by one as they entered Kastoria. They brought them to transport us.

The following day, without wasting any more time, the Germans threw us pell-mell into the trucks, kicking us, angrily shouting and beating us. It was cold. Snow was falling!

As we tried to compose ourselves and find someplace to sit, it dawned on us that the roof of the truck was covered by a thick canvas tied all around everywhere, so that from the outside, nobody could see us, or see the many SS continuously guarding us with guns.

Thus, in this frightful manner, they were irrevocably uprooting us and we were bidding goodbye to our native Kastoria forever. We left and were slowly moving farther and farther away, with anguished hearts, with black tears in our eyes, without knowing why we were being taken away, or where we were going.

After travelling a good many miles, we suddenly stopped someplace. It was to take on a group of 150 prisoners, captured here and there, to be added to our caravan.

During this transfer and alleged rest, a German came toward us, shouting. He began selecting four or five young girls. Among the first, he pointed his finger at my friend Paula Cohen and me. He took us, of course, by shouting commands in German that we didn't understand. Nevertheless, we obeyed submissively having no choice but to follow him.

He led us to a house. Arriving there, he made a motion for us to wait. He disappeared for a while, returning with buckets of water and mops. Motioning again as usual, he ordered us to clean the whole house in a hurry. (It must have been the house of a German commander.)

As soon as we understood what he wanted, we felt somewhat relieved because we had almost died of fear, expecting something worse to happen to us.

After finishing our work two or three hours later, he took us back to our people in the same manner. On the way, I recall, I walked over to Paula who was still trembling and asked her: "Paula, you're white as a ghost ... were you afraid they would kill us?"

"Yes, Berry dear, I'm still trembling, but I promise myself from now on, I'll stick close to my mama and never leave her side again."

I believe this event had such an impact on Paula, that later, upon entering Auschwitz, unwilling to be separated from her mom, she herself decided her own fate — to go with her mom into the crematorium.

Worried about their girls, when our people saw us coming back, they rushed over and asked what happened. We calmed them down, of course, telling them it was nothing to worry about, simply nothing — that we had only pretended to sweep and mop.

However, these were ominous signs, and the alarm bell of danger was continuously ringing in the ears of us all. But who heard it?

Curled up again inside the truck, we passed through villages and towns like lost souls, without food, without water. On the way, compassionate people, as well as representatives of the Red Cross, secretly tried to give us a little food from time to time. But the guards were on the lookout — trained Cerberuses — grabbing the food and

A Cry for Tomorrow 76859 ...

mercilessly throwing it to the dogs, mocking both the donors and us.

Harmankió ghetto

Exhausted by hunger and fatigue, we arrived at a suburb of Thessaloniki called "Harmankió" — at a camp having a long, narrow barrack and a huge yard encircled by barbed wire like a large building site.

They shoved us in and closed the wire doors behind us, leaving armed guards beside them. As soon as we got in, everybody rushed to find a place, a corner of their own to accommodate the babies, the sick, the elderly and their few belongings.

After a short while, a few went out to the yard to breathe fresh air. Still dazed by all that was happening to us, we looked around, trying to compose ourselves and comprehend our situation. We met each other again ... gazed at each other full of anxiety ... talked amongst ourselves. It was unbelievable. What would become of us?

"There is plenty of cold water running from a tap in the yard," someone announced. So we all ran at the same time to refresh our faces, wash our hands, and later on, change the babies and infants. Even we adults somehow washed ourselves.

Men and women rushed to queue and quickly wash their things, their clothes and those of their families as best they could. One helped the other.

Then a so-called mess arrived: a thin soup and a little bread which they gave us as we queued, one behind the other.

The following day, as I recall, the place filled with more prisoners — Athenians — who were caught during exactly the same period, and transported here to join us. We passed the time asking one another which part of Greece one had come from, and how one was caught, etc. Always the same circumstances and always the same reason: They were Jews, deported just like us and facing the same fate.

Outside the fenced area on the opposite hill, we could see a crowd of people. Christian friends had come to find persons they knew among us. They shouted various names. Being so far away, we, at least, couldn't distinguish them. Our friend Theano Kovatse (classmate of Lena Eliaou, Rebecca Pissirilou, and Rebecca Zaharia) was a student at the University of Thessaloniki at that time. Just as we were discussing her, someone said she herself had come to find us there, but we couldn't see her from such a distance.

Every morning guards selected several strongly built men, took them out and brought them back in the evening. They worked somewhere or brought food for approximately 1,500 people, and the number constantly increased.

During this period we would go outside in the yard and walk, spending time with one another, especially relatives and friends. One day I noticed my close friend and neighbor, Rebecca (Pissirilou) Franko, clinging to her husband and mother. She was not speaking, her belly was protruding, and being in her ninth month, she couldn't even lift her feet from the weight. She was expecting any day. We came up to her, just to say an encouraging word. We were all worried about her.

The following day, the International Red Cross appeared and to our relief, after a great deal of trouble, they managed to take her out with them. She was in labor, but in this difficult circumstance, they separated her from her husband, mother, father, and entire family. Nobody of her own was allowed to accompany her. Despite the pregnant woman's pleading and that of her husband's, they took her out alone and transported her to a clinic.

At that time the Red Cross announced something new! Anyone by chance having Spanish or Turkish nationality was to come forward and leave the ghetto.

We stared at one another.... "No," my father said. "We are Hellenes, we don't have any foreign nationality whatsoever, nor should we claim any."

Suddenly a family came forward, shouting that by chance their father was from Smyrna. They said he settled in Kastoria as a young man, and had raised a family there. Not by choice, his old citizenship had remained Turkish. His name was Leon Misrahi. I recall he had a tic, sniffing every other minute. A kind man, he was my private French teacher and I knew him very well. After showing various papers he carried on him, he took his entire family out and left for Thessaloniki, free. What a stroke of luck!

The next moment, we heard another voice from inside the yard — that of Leon Faratzi, a young good-looking blond man about twenty-one years of age, who had come to Kastoria with the group of Yugoslavians. He showed his papers, shouted, ran up and down, and sure enough, was out free as well.

Bravo Leon Faratzi! You succeeded again, I said to myself smiling as I remembered the good old days in Kastoria — a few months ago that is — when he waltzed with us and danced the new dances at our

parties. Light on his feet, tall, witty, and very dexterous at everything
— just like now, dexterous at leaving.

They were going out free and we envied them. Everyone at that time was following his own destiny, and those who left the ghetto did not know nor could ever imagine what would have been waiting for them!

Still in Harmankió

Walking aimlessly and restlessly in the yard of the camp and arriving at the backside where the barrack ends, I suddenly became aware of a hole! The barbed wire fence at that spot had been cut, leaving an opening through which one could get out. It seemed that other prisoners before us had opened it and surely, someone wisely must have escaped to the outside. I went closer. Stopped. Examining it carefully, I began calculating its dimensions. Could I fit in that hole, I wondered? And then, could one easily get out the other side? My mind got busy and in my imagination I began seeing myself going in and out many times, sometimes with deep scratches from the barbed wires, bleeding; sometimes wedged in and trapped, unable to move ... God, my mind concentrated on this idea for hours.

I grew worried and anxious. Surely, somebody would first have to push me from the inside. If I finally managed to get out, I'd go to Thessaloniki. But I didn't know anyone there who could help me. How would I manage all by myself where everything's strange? At that moment I felt paralyzed, unable to move. This time too I didn't dare. It was my last chance to escape.

The Road to Auschwitz

In the trains

When they suddenly announced we were leaving Thessaloniki, my morale reached a new low because we were forsaking Greece for good. It was April 1, 1944 — departure. With the sacks on my shoulder, I gazed sadly around, this time looking for some warm support that I badly needed. Everybody was already a human rag in a worse state than I was. We moved toward the railway station without strength, without resistance, like automata — as a flock — with the dogs barking at our heels.

It was the first of April, the beginning of spring, but even nature was mirroring our condition, lamenting our fate. The atmosphere was nasty. Black clouds hung low irritating our faces, and the cold coupled with our fear made us shudder and shiver to our bones. Loud puffing of steam engines pierced our ears! The trains ... yes, the trains ... the wagons ... so many wagons.

These wagons were intended for animals, so they couldn't possibly be putting us in there! Yet, before long, they pushed me like an animal, shouting to quickly get up into one.

A hail of orders came from the SS: "Hurry up, move inside. Yes, one after another, move forward, crowd in with the other 20, 30 ... 40, make room for more in the same one ... 60, 80."

"But there's no room for more ... *there's no more room!*" In a few moments eighty persons were squeezed in one on top of the other. We found ourselves inside a wagon, and could hear the chains and bolts outside hermetically locking us in! Twelve such wagons were loaded with lightening speed and the train grew longer as more wagons from the south were coupled on.

I found myself closed in and immobilized somewhere, without being able to move. "Claustrophobia, asphyxia," I cried, frightened, suffocating. "I can't," somebody else shouted. Panic reigned! One could only see wide-open eyes and frantic hands being raised seeking salvation.

A Cry for Tomorrow 76859 ...

Somehow I slowly managed to push my arms a little away from my body to relieve the pressure ... I was still suffocating, sweating.... In the same wagon some distance away I recognized Dora; further on her brother; at the other end in the middle of the crowd, my Uncle Zahos. What a calamity!

The three of them, pushing and shoving this way and that, reached me after great difficulty. "There," I said gasping for breath, "let's slowly move over there, near the vent to get some air." A little further on, directly above our heads, was a wire-netted square opening serving as the only "window." Fortunately, being rather tall, my head got somewhat close to the window and I felt a little relief breathing in some air, but only for a few moments. We had to give our place to others who in the meantime were fainting and screaming for air.

After a while I found another place and tried to pull myself together. "My family?" I asked myself. "God only knows where they are. They got on other wagons, no doubt. The young ones must be crying. Can grandpa and grandma endure this? My poor brother Alberto, where could he be?" My mind flew to them now and my eyes filled with tears.

At that moment Dora came close to me, took my arm and said, "Courage, Berry, it's only the beginning for us!"

"What! What are you saying? Can there be this much wickedness and barbarism? Where do the Germans find this rage? Aren't they human beings made of the same clay as we ... or are they beasts masquerading in human form?"

"Unfortunately, they are humans made of the same clay as we are," Dora said. "Apparently we have all been carrying the beast inside us for thousands of millions of years, ever since primitive times. But this beast, if not tamed at the proper time, risks ruling us, taking us back to the jungle again."

"Such beastly instincts can't possibly exist in all of us. I don't want to believe that. Where's civility? Civilized life? Where are we? Where are we going?"

"Can't you see? Where they're taking us civilization no longer exists. Be prepared from now on. Be brave. You'll need all your strength. Above all, keep your morale high. That's the most important thing, so we don't lose our humanity as well. We must understand that these people out there are laying a bet. They want to humiliate us and reduce us, until we become demoralized and cease feeling like human beings. Berry dear, you must learn to endure, you must!"

The Road to Auschwitz

I looked at Dora, hypnotized. Her words were even more powerful than the situation itself! My God, what else is in store for us? I felt the injustice and started crying and screaming: "Why? But why, what have we done to them? What have I done to them?"

It was a wailing "why" which has never been answered.

The train, now at full steam, was scattering our shouts and cries everywhere — through the forests, over the prairies, on the rivers we crossed and left behind. But nobody heard us. Was the whole world deaf at that time?

Our train ran on for hours and hours, non-stop until it reached Yugoslavia. At the border between Bulgaria and Yugoslavia they finally decided to open the doors. In sudden panic, one shoving the other, we rushed to get out, to jump down, to reach the ground and breathe fresh air.

"Back inside, back inside!" the Germans started shouting. "Get the dead out first!"

Indeed, they were the first victims who didn't survive even the first torment. Poor wretched people ... what a swift end. But how lucky they were.

We had to separate from them unceremoniously in great haste, and bury them there in makeshift fashion. We didn't have time for either sorrow or the comprehension that they were dead.

"Quickly, quickly. And empty the slop pails!" they shouted.

In a corner of the wagon we had set up our improvised toilet: a blanket hanging from up above covered the slop pail where eighty people by turn went to relieve their bodily needs. The slop pail had long since overflowed, and the smell was unbearable and choking. We couldn't stand it any longer. Fortunately, it would now be emptied. Several young hands grabbed it and the slop pail was emptied quickly, cleaned as best it could be, and put in its place again in the same corner. Everything had to be done in a hurry because they said we wouldn't be staying out of the wagon more than one or two hours. We barely had time to see one another, ask about each other, stretch our arms and legs. Breathe!

Suddenly I heard some of our people from the other wagons shouting in Italian: *"Luigi, Mikelo, Pietro, cosa fate qui?"*

What were they doing here? How could these Italians — people whom we knew — be in this remote place? Then they themselves explained how in early September 1943, after Italy surrendered, the Germans took the Italians prisoner and brought them here to work on the railroad.

They recognized us as well and seeing our unacceptable condition, felt sorry for us. After everyone's initial surprise, they searched their sacks, taking out whatever items they could. Then they distributed them secretly so the Germans wouldn't notice. We cried from gratitude.

We bid them heartfelt good-byes as we quickly got up into the cattle wagons again to continue on. Second stop: Hungary! No, there they didn't open the doors. They kept us in while the train remained stopped for hours. For a moment we hoped, but unfortunately, the train just moved backwards and forwards a little, and finally left for Vienna.

Now and then I could see out of the little window vent again. I saw the fields, the trees, the green world outside that we were crossing. How beautiful nature is, I thought. Look, the Danube no doubt. Yes, it must be that river and all we once learned about in geography. What a dream to enjoy under different circumstances! But now, what could one think about or appreciate?

Another stop. We arrived in Vienna! But they didn't open the doors. We just sat there! Directly opposite, just a short distance away was a fountain flowing with gurgling water, abundant water, water, so much water its sound annoyingly buzzed in our ears. Our thirst was unbearable and with every passing minute our throats became drier and drier. Our lips were dry and chapped and our tongues dry as well, and the water in front of us running continuously aggravated our thirst even more.

Thirst is a horrible feeling, maybe worse than hunger! One could hear frantic cries coming from all the wagons! *"Wasser, Wasser, bitte!"* — Water, water, please! I saw my uncle Zahos take off his beautiful red tie and offer it from the window for some water. No response. It was as if we didn't exist. Yet there in the park, which we could see from our little window, Viennese mothers were pushing their little children in strollers, quietly and nicely. We had children with mothers exactly like them in each of our wagons ... but our children were screaming loudly and turning blue from crying because they needed water.

Indifferent to the wailing they heard from our wagons, the Viennese mothers didn't even glance toward us. Their life, their world had no connection with ours — it was all theirs, belonging exclusively to them. Our little ones were crying more and more, louder and louder. They couldn't tolerate their thirst any longer. It was unbearable. I shall never forget mama Bértitse, a strong, young Yugoslavian woman who was with us in the wagon with two small children. At that moment she had her little child pee in a cup which she took out of her sack, and after a bit, offered it to him to drink as water.

"Ach, Bértitse, what are you doing?"

"It doesn't matter," she said. "It's his after all, coming from his clean little body. I can't take it anymore, I can't bear listening to him cry and scream." And the little child drank his pee, because he was thirsty, terribly thirsty.

The days passed, each one worse than the last. At night we lay down in rows like sardines — one almost on top of the other — many times in shifts, because there was not enough room for everyone at the same time. Curled up with our eyes closed, we followed the voices of the Germans and the whistling of the train. A bad feeling has stayed with me to this day. Even now when I hear train whistles, I connect them to the Germans and that train. An anxiety and an agony comes over me similar to what I felt then, when we were wondering: What will the Germans decide for us today or what will happen tomorrow? Will the wagon doors open? Will they give us water? Will they take us out for good? It was an endless ordeal that became worse and worse and exhausted us day after day, until April 11, 1944, arrived — a fateful day.

It was about 10:00 a.m., if I remember well, when Dora's brother came over to me and started saying something. That he liked me very much ... that he would be happy when we got out to....

I couldn't hear what he was saying. I just looked him straight in the eye, noticing that he was not joking, poor guy, and that he resolutely, how can I say, was waiting very seriously for my answer.

But, I thought to myself, is he so sure we're going to be free out there? Or is he completely mad? Can he seriously be thinking and showing these kinds of feelings, now at such moments? How could he find them? How? I opened my mouth to say something negative to him, but then, I remember, I was trying to soften what I was going to say, not to offend him. And I stayed like that with my mouth open ... because the doors of our train groaned. Yes, the doors of the train finally opened, at that exact moment — in Auschwitz.

Auschwitz

Auschwitz Station

It was a gray winter day when we got off the train, dragging our sacks, this time without strength after interminable days closed in the wagons. I remember the SS in their long, warm overcoats, armed like rulers, commandingly giving out orders, and I remember myself jumping out of the wagon, hungry, exhausted! Then the queues, and SS shouting for interpreters among us who could translate German.

Everything had to be understood quickly and we had to obey without any resistance. Bértitse, the educated Yugoslavian from Belgrade offered first, and readily translated whatever they said.

"Leave all your belongings here," she said. "You'll find them upon returning from the bath you'll be taking soon. All elderly and sick; pregnant women; mothers with small children; old and disabled — get up on the big trucks immediately for transfer to your 'destination.' Don't be afraid. Go quickly."

For a moment, I couldn't bear listening anymore to what was being said, because I was intently looking around to find a relative among the people still coming down from the train. Finally, I suddenly saw my brother (three years younger than I) obediently putting his sack onto a pile. I let out an agonized piercing shout!

"Alberto, Alberto, keep your sack! Don't believe them. How will you possibly find it again in that pile? Pay no attention. Take it with you, or you'll end up without clothes!"

He raised his eyes toward me and seemed to recognize me, but had neither time to reply, nor say anything. SS were already pushing him, and seconds later I couldn't see him anymore — he had disappeared.

Which way did he go? I remember him leaving without his clothes. I stood there feeling bitter, and worry gnawed at me. And to think how I had prepared each and every piece, I said to myself. Then from my hands they grabbed my sack and suddenly I'm shoved face-to-face with a high ranking military officer who tells me in an authoritative and pressing way: "You — get in that line. You'll go on foot ... you're young, strong, understand?"

Hell no to understanding.... Why are they separating us like this?

To others he said: "You, up. Get up into the truck quickly. You, go to the line. You up. You down."

Why are they sorting us? What are they doing now? Bértitse explained and explained and translated. And when she finished, they said to her: "You now, get in the line to walk. Thank you for your services."

"No," replied Bértitse. "My children are already in the trucks and they're crying without me."

"Join the line quickly we're telling you ... you'll see them again later."

"Impossible! I won't leave them for a second. Please ... I beg you. Don't do this to me. I'll go crazy. Let me go with them."

When they finally understood she wouldn't yield, they said to her: "Go where you want, you asked for it." They didn't have time to lose. Relieved, she got up on the truck, clasping her two little children tightly in her arms as it left.

Still confused, I dragged myself like an automaton toward the line, as they advised me to do, and searched for Dora and the other girls.

"Dora, are you here too? Come close to me so we'll be together."

I hardly finished my phrase when I saw a truck full of my relatives passing right by me. Oh, my daddy, holding my four small brothers and sisters between his knees, and beside him my stepmother.

"Dora, I'm leaving," I said. "I can't come with you, I'm sorry. I'm going to help my father who needs me now. Look! Do you see him?"

At once, I stepped out of the line, and being very agile, jumped on the truck's big black tire. I quickly set one foot on the tire — ready in a second to follow with the other, which was already in the air — when I felt a hard slap in the face and saw stars. The blow was so strong it threw me to the ground one metre away.

"What happened to me? Who beat me so ruthlessly?"

My cheek was burning, my ear still ringing and my whole body hurting. Why this so suddenly? I want to go to my daddy — only that — this minute. I raised my eyes and was confronted by "someone"

AUSCHWITZ

ordering me and threatening me, his finger pointing to the line where Dora was. There and only there was I to go. His eyes gave me little choice. And if I dared disobey, God help me. For a moment I thought he would kill me. In spite of everything, I tried to leave again because I was wild with anger. I was stubborn, but I could feel he was even more stubborn than I. At that moment, I heard my father's loud voice begging me: "Please, don't come here, obey them. I can't bear to see them beating you. Do you hear, my child? Obey them." I raised my eyes despairingly toward my father, and saw he was full of pain for me! My poor, sweet father, what you must witness! And these were the last words I would hear from him for I was never to see him again.

I turned, forcing myself back to the line again, next to Dora, only in order to obey my daddy because I felt he wanted me to. "Give me your hand, Dora," I said to her, "and tell me you'll never ever leave me." So I stayed close to her, not leaving the line anymore, watching the whole tragic scene.

The huge square was surrounded by SS armed guards. At that moment, the most horrible human drama of the Twentieth Century was unfolding. We were approximately 1,500 people being evaluated, considered, judged, so that a few young boys and girls could be selected and singled out into two lines for work.

And I was now in line among those few, unable even to suspect the hideous reality.

Speechless, I stared from afar at the black tire of the truck that took my family and nearly took me as it slowly moved away and disappeared. That tire would stay with me like a dark nightmare for the rest of my life.

I also saw many other trucks leaving, one behind the other full of human souls. The last one ... there ... passing right next to me, I still see it before me even now — two little blue eyes, a little blond head with beautiful curls, and a little hand waving and sending me kisses. This last "good-bye" of my little cousin only six years old will accompany me all my life, as long as I envision again and again this same scene before me — the hour of *Selektion* at Auschwitz Station, there by the trains.

The *Selektion?* They separated people inhumanely and mercilessly for two different directions: existence or annihilation. The one to life and the other to death. The trucks went directly to the crematoria. The people on them had to die because they were useless and didn't have the right to exist. And the few young people in the two lines would soon enter Auschwitz concentration camp.* There to provide work as forced labor for a few days, a few weeks, a few months, for however long they could endure this camp.

Auschwitz

"Labor Makes [You] Free" was written high above in German: *ARBEIT MACHT FREI*.

Stepping through the iron gate from the square, the two separate lines of young people (320 men and 113 women) were ordered to start walking. Leading us in front were guides, and behind us armed German soldiers holding chains in their hands leashed to German shepherd dogs. The more we advanced, the more we felt deserted and isolated. The further we moved inside, the more we became alienated from the outside world.

From time to time during our march, we met groups of badly dressed people wearing striped uniforms of hopsack, who looked at us oddly, as if we were coming from a remote planet which they had

---

*On April 27, 1940, on the orders of Reichsführer Heinrich Himmler, a concentration camp was created in Oswiecim, (Auschwitz) Poland, between Krakow and Katovitze (areas occupied by the Nazis).

The SS Hauptsturmbannführer Rudolf Hoess was appointed military commander of the camp and from June 14, 1940, the first trains arrived. In the beginning, only Polish prisoners reached the camp. In 1941, the Nazis sent Czechs, Yugoslavians, Austrians, Germans (who were anti-regime), even Russian prisoners of war. Later, French, Dutch, Greeks, Hungarians arrived and Gypsies from Russia, Norway, Romania, and Italy, about 405,000 men and women.

Himmler, at a meeting with the military commander Hoess, reported that "the existing extermination centers in the eastern zones do not suffice for our plans. This is why I chose Auschwitz, first for its convenient position for transport and, second, because it is isolated and camouflaged beyond any suspicion." Thus, he immediately sent a specialist, SS Obersturmbannführer Adolf Eichmann, who, as soon as he arrived in Auschwitz, informed commander Hoess on the extermination plans.

(From Auschwitz Museum Archives)

1,500 prisoners were brought to the Auschwitz concentration camp on April 11, 1944 from Athens and Kastoria, Greece. Of the 1,500 Jews brought to the camp that day, only 320 men and 113 women were selected for work. The other 1,067 were killed in the gas chambers. The selected women received numbers from 76856 to 77183. The number on my arm is 76859, so I was apparently the fourth in line.

These facts are recorded in a document I personally brought from Auschwitz, when on April 26, 1987, I went on a pilgrimage to Auschwitz-Birkenau for the first time after forty-three years. This pilgrimage was organized under the auspices of the Central Jewish Council.

once known. But they themselves also looked strange, indeed. They didn't look human. They were feeble skeletons with shaved heads and sunken eyes.

I didn't dare dwell on it, neither did I want to draw premature conclusions. To shun this deplorable scene before me, I looked around searching for a bit of nature. There wasn't any. The footpath was endless and the area around us for miles was barren. As far as the eye could see there was continuous precisely strung barbed wire that divided the immense space into smaller areas.

For a moment I felt lost! The only familiar things in this ugly, cold environment were those few girls from the same town and country, walking together having the same fate.

Our boys in the other line suddenly changed direction ... no doubt being led somewhere nearby, but we couldn't see them anymore. Would we see them again, I wondered, not even noticing who they took out from the line. Anyway it didn't matter ... since we all came here together, I thought, we'll surely meet again.

And the *chimneys!* The only "décor" in this entire remote place. The chimneys were very tall, with mouths spewing giant flames towards the sky. Oh God, what an unpleasant smell! What could be burning in those chimneys that the smell comes all the way here and irritates our nostrils?

Finally, we stopped at a women's camp of enormous dimensions. It had long narrow barracks with corridors in perfect geometric layout and was very crowded. This time, volunteer interpreters were available — women dressed in the white and blue-gray striped clothes, their heads almost completely shaven. They asked which language we preferred: Greek, Spanish, German, Russian, Italian — whatever one wished of every nationality.

"No, don't go into the barrack yet," they told us, "you must first get a number. Get in line quickly."

When my turn came, a rather young girl took charge of me who suddenly said: "Give me your left arm. Over here by your wrist, I'll etch a number — a tattoo — and remember it all your life if you live and for as long as you live. I'll try to make the number as small as possible so it won't look ugly." She immediately began pricking my arm with a syringe full of ink, little by little trying not to hurt me ... until she marked: "76859" with a triangle underneath. That half Star of David meant I was a Jew, and besides, it was the only charge against me.

A Cry for Tomorrow 76859 ...

"I'm a Jew too," she told me, "but now, after so many years here I've become a *Kapo*."

I didn't understand what she meant. She'll make a "small number." I must remember it "if I live and as long as I live"; that "she's a *Kapo*," etc. Despite her being careful, it hurt all the while she tattooed this awful number on my arm. But anyway, what's this all about? How shall I always remember it? Won't this number fade away tomorrow?

As the girl finished with me, another one took over who was holding scissors and a shaver in her hands. "Bend over," this other girl told me, "you're tall and I can't reach to cut your hair." Then she cut it haphazardly, any old way.

"Hurry up, get in the barracks now," they repeated. "Undress, take off everything, naked as when you were born, and hand over to us whatever you take off. All of it — panties, stockings, shoes, everything. We'll bring you other clothes directly from the kiln and these will be your only camp clothes."

Very embarrassed and with great reluctance, we disrobed and waited, standing stark naked for hours, shivering. Finally, when the clothes arrived from the kiln, they handed me a package tied with a belt. The package was still damp with steam from the sauna and inside was a worn dress with fresh bloodstains still smelling; one piece of underwear (panty-like bloomers); and mixed in together, two shoes, I remember well ... one, a man's shoe and the other, a woman's shoe.

"Put them on, be quick about it, and go outside to the line, five-five to a row so we can count you."

I just couldn't put them on me ... the blood on my dress made me nauseous, and all the rest didn't fit, no matter what. Is it possible? A man's shoe and a woman's shoe! How can I wear them?

"Put them on quickly, or else!" German SS shouted, starting to mercilessly beat whomever they could with belts.

"From now on forget your name!" they screamed. "Memorize the number on your arm. You, number 76859, you'll pronounce it this way: *"sechsundsiebzig, achthundert, neunundfünfzig.* Repeat it over and over, each one your own number, you animals, *verfluchte Juden."*

A few minutes later, transformed circus-like, they pushed us out for the first *Appell* or "roll-call," as we were arranged in rows of five. We looked freakish! I could not recognize anybody, not even myself.

They counted and recounted us, and when they finished, two or three small pots of soup arrived which they portioned out, one cup

Auschwitz

My father

My mother Vedoura and my father Israel Kassouto

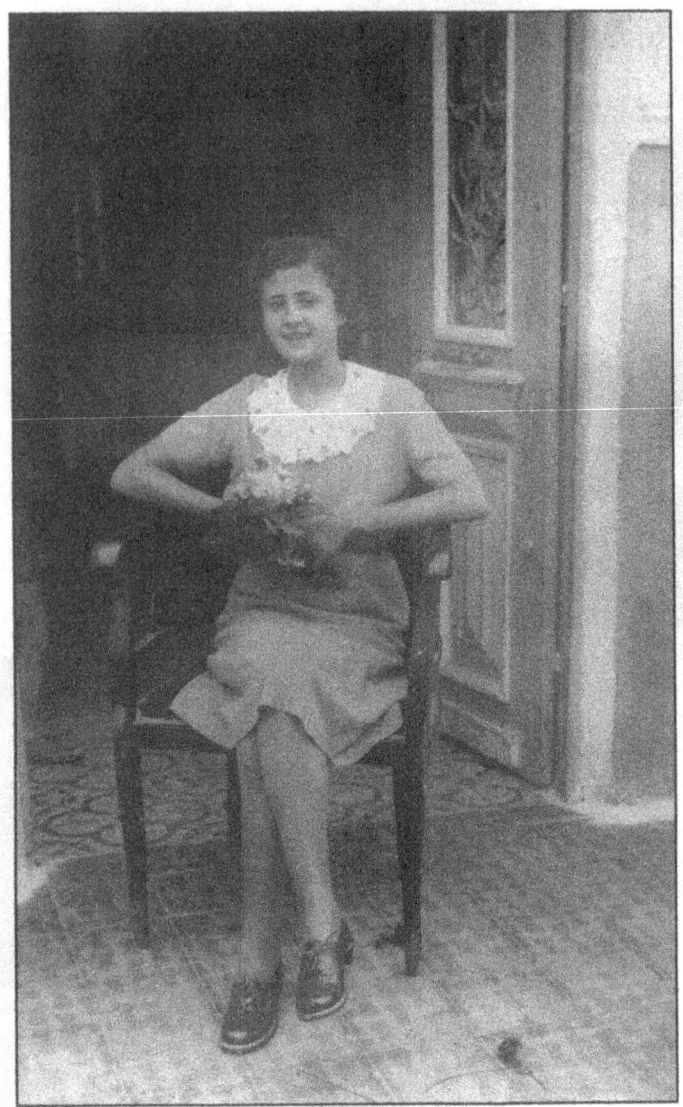

In Kastoria

AUSCHWITZ

Seated, my paternal grandparents Jacob Cassuto and Boenna Cassuto. Standing, my uncle Gouzel Cassuto and his wife Rebecca. Foreground, Gourel and Rebecca's daughter, Bonica, who blew me kisses from the truck as it was leaving for the gas chamber.

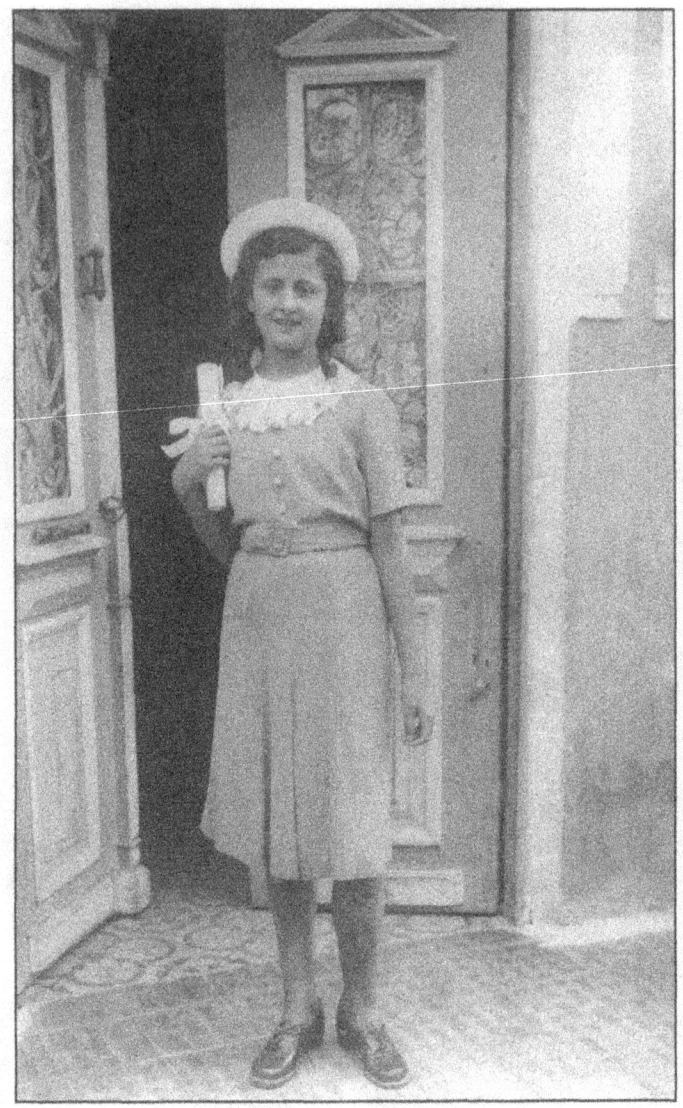

The entrance of my house in Kastoria

AUSCHWITZ

At the ghetto of Thessaloniki

A CRY FOR TOMORROW 76859 ...

The last chance to escape

AUSCHWITZ

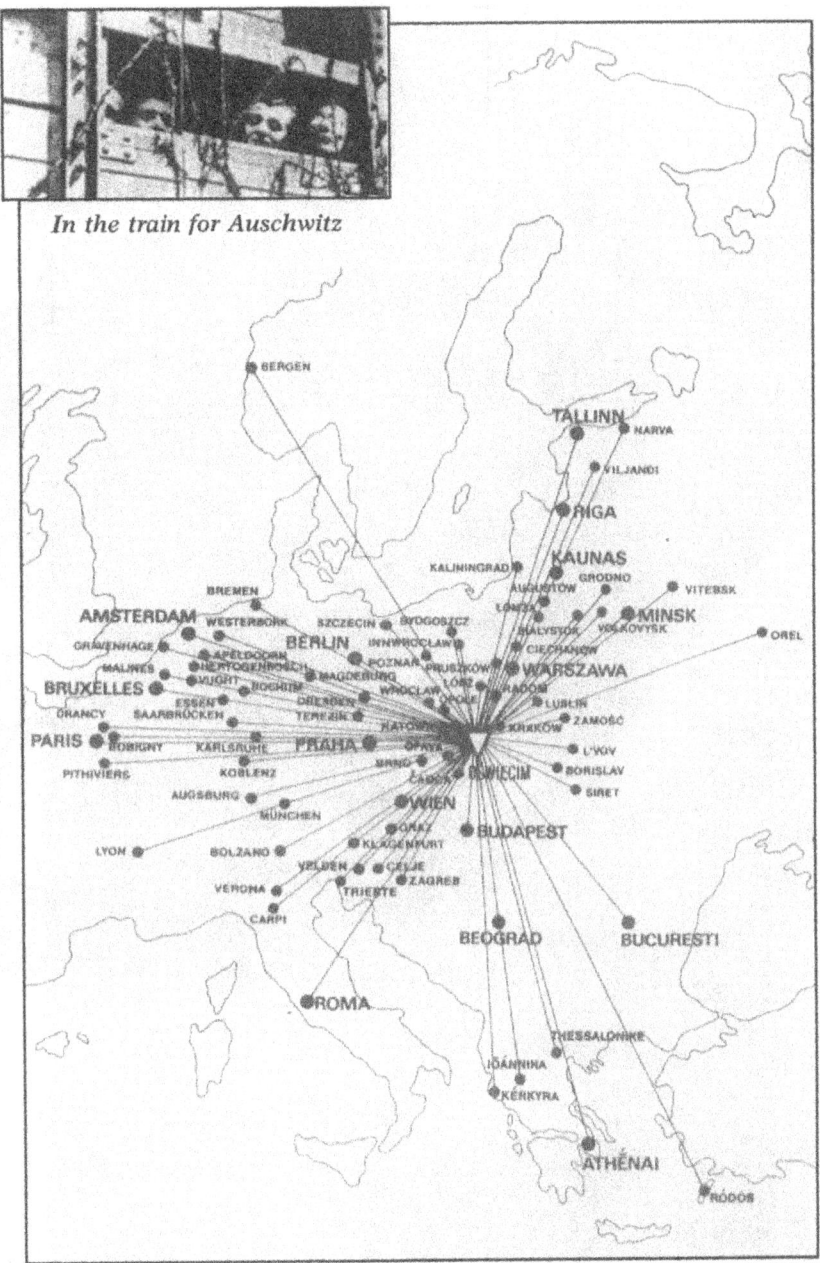

In the train for Auschwitz

Railroad lines leading the Jews of Europe to the camps

A Cry for Tomorrow 76859 ...

Auschwitz

Station

A Cry for Tomorrow 76859 ...

Selection at Auschwitz Station

Auschwitz

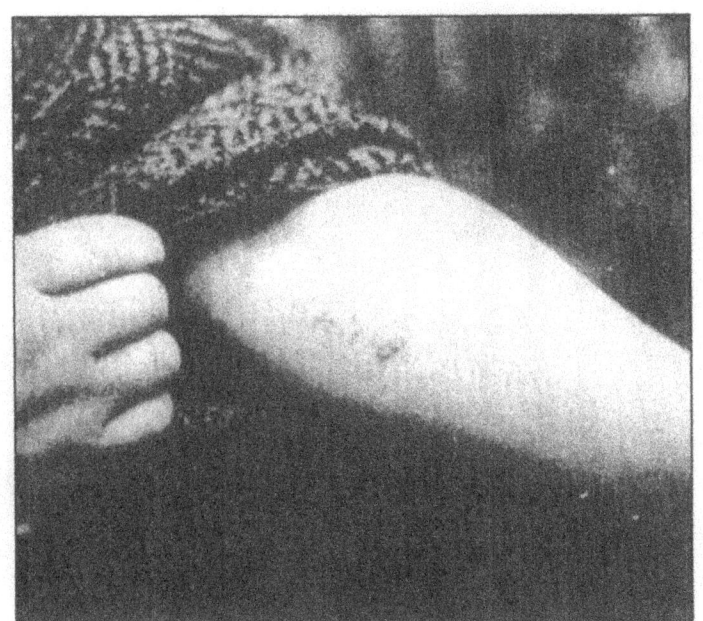

The tattooed number

The entrance to the camp: "Work Brings You Freedom"

AUSCHWITZ

The electrified fence surrounding the camp

A Cry for Tomorrow 76859 ...

Auschwitz-Berkenau

Block 11, known as "Block of Death"

A Cry for Tomorrow 76859 ...

The daily meal

per person. It was a blackish slop. Despite being extremely hungry, that dirty liquid disgusted me. I looked at it a long time, holding the cup in my hands, not having the courage to put it to my mouth.

I felt completely lost by what was happening to us. They threatened us with death, sadism, brutality. They were destroying our personality and feeding us worse than animals.

I was shattered inside, ready to collapse ... when I heard Dora's voice shouting loudly at me, trying to shake me out of it: "Berry! Take your portion of bread. This small piece is for the whole day and night." Dora had grabbed the piece of bread handed out for two. (They distributed bread deliberately like that, for us to cut in two ourselves, so people would fight amongst themselves.) Many times we had to divide it in six.

"Take your portion," she said, giving me the bigger of the two.

Only then was she able to bring me back to reality. Immediately I said to her: "But, I don't think you cut it equally. You gave me more ... why did you do that?"

"Because I know how to live on less bread, while you're not strong enough. I see it — you've surrendered."

"But don't you see how they've reduced us? Why did they take our good clothes and dress us in these rags? Why do they humiliate us like this? Here, look, I've a man's shoe and a woman's. They've even cut our hair!" I couldn't stop crying!

"So what?" she replied calmly with exquisite courage. "If you're strong, nobody can humiliate you. Raise up your shoulders. Courage. Keep your morale high."

"And where shall I find the strength, when they only give us a tiny piece of bread a day? Don't you see?"

"Take my portion too. It's not the bread that will save you. Every one of us has a great reservoir of strength. Find it. Search for it. Tenaciously. If you want to save yourself, you'll find it. It's inside you."

In this tragic moment of my life I discovered my guardian angel, my guru. She imparted an iron and unyielding will to me and tried to persuade me that I had to live.

"Cut the bread again equally, I have strength just like you," I responded. "I'll endure, you'll see."

"I hope so," Dora said ... unconvinced.

For me it was a very important moment, and I didn't quite believe it myself either. Oh God ... as long as I don't weaken again.

We entered Barrack No. 27. The barracks were called "blocks."

A Cry for Tomorrow 76859 ...

Auschwitz and Birkenau had twenty-five such blocks, and each had a separate number. Number 9, 10, 11, 19, 20, 21, 27, 28, etc. Each block had its *Blockoberst,* its leader. She was a prisoner herself, appointed by the SS, responsible for disciplining the other prisoners and for the cleanliness of the block. If they found she was not obeying their orders, they would relieve her of her position as *Blockoberst* and punish her.

We entered the "Quarantine Block" for new arrivals where we would remain for forty days. Our *Blockoberst,* named Daisy, was a Greek woman from Thessaloniki. For a moment we were happy, thinking we would speak in Greek with her and ask her to inform us on our situation, especially about when we were going to meet the rest of our family, our parents, brothers, sisters, and relatives....

She replied bluntly that it was too soon for us to learn any details, and that the following day we would find out with our own eyes what the reality was.

"Now," she said, "you must sleep early, because at nine o'clock in the evening all lights are switched off and nobody is allowed to circulate, not even to go to the toilet. Very early tomorrow, at four-thirty, you will hear the first bell which is the rousing call. You must quickly make up your beds and at five, with the second bell that you will hear, you must be dressed and ready to go out for *Appell,* or 'roll-call' five-five in your line. *Appell* is repeated regularly in the evening at seven o'clock, but it may be repeated several times a day."

"Here in the camp, it's no laughing matter. You must obey and above all, for your own sake, you must join a *Kommando,* a work gang, otherwise, God help you."

Then she showed us the dormitory, a room on the ground floor with approximately eighty, three-storied bunk beds, one on top of the other. Each bed had a straw mattress with one blanket — very rarely two — where three or four girls had to sleep together, all sharing the same blanket. In the attic there were fewer beds, arranged in the same way as on the ground floor.

I laid down on the edge of one of the bottom beds, which I chose quickly, before they might force me to go up to a top bed. I thought it would be more convenient to be below, in order to jump out readily and quickly, in case of an emergency.

I was shivering from the cold, and tried to warm myself by the breath of the girl next to me, asking the other three to leave me a little of the blanket. I put my hands under my head, imagining it was a pillow, which of course did not exist.

I don't remember whether I slept at all that night. In the dark, I tried to guess what terrible things were in store for us! Soon I heard the first bell that frightened us all, and at once we got up.

Some girls were looking for their wooden shoes, others for the piece of bread they had hidden for the following day but couldn't find, screaming in desperation. The commotion continued until two or three Polish women (not Jews) came in to impose order, holding whips in their hands that fell on us like birds of prey. Beating and beating us, you didn't know which direction the blows were coming from.

I wasn't paying attention to the second bell, so two Greek women pushed me out for *Appell*. They must have been there a year already (since 1943), having come from Thessaloniki. I tried smiling at one of these girls, asking her in Greek what her name was and what was happening here.

"Don't talk now. Get in the line with the newcomers until they count us. Then I'll tell you everything," she said.

I stood still, waiting patiently for the SS to finish counting us over and over. It took a half-hour for them to verify that nobody was missing, either from the old-timers or the new arrivals. The number of prisoners of each block was systematically recorded in a book and in this way, the SS were able to determine at each *Appell* whether there was an absence, or a death (or an escape which had to be reported immediately by the *Blockoberst*).

The old-timers stood in a line opposite us and were in very bad shape. Young girls 18, 20, 25, and 30 years of age looked like wizened old women of 100 years. Their feet and hands were full of wounds and boils. They were bent double from weakness, and could hardly drag their feet.

"My name is Rachel," said a young dark girl, her hair completely shaved off. "How beautiful you still look," she said, "fat, fat, plump, newly brought here directly from your home."

At that time I was rather slim by Greek standards, but Rachel, however, was right to think I was fat and plump!

"That's how I was too, like you, when I arrived here," she said. "I imagine that until yesterday you ate as much as you wanted, even chocolates, sweets, anything you wished. Don't tell me it's a lie.... Now what do you want to know? Where your relatives are since you separated yesterday? Come look ... see those chimneys over there spitting flames and smoke? Don't you smell burned flesh? Well, it's

A Cry for Tomorrow 76859 ...

their smell. They've passed up through there. They've burned them! And they'll burn others. Every day they burn, and sooner or later they'll burn you and perhaps me ... we'll all pass through there."

I looked at her frightened and at the same time I was shaken up having met a crazy woman who had completely lost her mind and didn't know what she was saying. It just couldn't be true!

"Yes, I know, you think I'm crazy. That's exactly what I thought when I first came here a year ago. But it's the bitter truth! Want to or not you'll believe it. You'll see for yourself. And what's more ... here, never pretend you are sick, it'll be your end. They don't keep the sick alive here, they burn them ... and when the 'transports' don't arrive, that is the trains from Europe, then they collect some of us here and make *Selektionen* for the furnace. The furnaces are called 'crematoria' and these crematoria have to burn six, seven, sometimes ten thousand a day. You went through the first *Selektion* already yesterday. You didn't know it, of course, but from now on though you'll learn. You'll see how many *Selektionen* you still have to pass through ... as long as you live.

And listen carefully to what I tell you now. Do you see that barbed wire? For God's sake don't touch it because it's electrified. If you disturb it you'll be electrocuted and die. Only if you want to commit suicide ... then do it. And I'm sure that one day you'll want to, as you won't be able to endure the life in this camp."

All at once I closed my ears with both my hands. No ... I didn't want to hear anything more, even if they were the fantasies of a raving mad woman!

I quickly left her side and looked for the girls from Greece ... to tell them. But what could I tell them? They were crying and shaking uncontrollably. They learned from the older prisoners what I had just heard.

It must be true. They all say it — even Daisy the *Blockoberst* said it. Besides, one could see it for oneself: the chimneys full of flames, the smell of burned flesh, every fifty meters an SS guard, and every guard placed on a watchtower twelve to twenty meters high to watch the camp's block houses from above. One could see permanent patrols in parallel lines (which ran for forty kilometers), making any attempt at escape virtually impossible. Indeed, the SS force totalled 8,000 to 10,000 men. How could one escape their attention?

Terrified, we asked, "Where are we? Where have they brought us?"

"To the Birkenau and Auschwitz camps which are forty miles from Cracow," somebody replied. "It is very cold in winter here,

AUSCHWITZ

sometimes 15 to 20 degrees below zero, and it's very difficult to survive in such cold weather. On the other hand, in summer the sun is unbearable!"

"What kind of camp is Birkenau, and what is Auschwitz?" we asked again.

"In Birkenau where we are now, are our dormitories, and the main productive work is stone. Nearby is a vast stone area. Most likely they will send you newcomers to work there. It's not far from here, but it's rather hard work.

"The production at Auschwitz is death. Everything is perfectly designed for the operation of the crematoria. Moreover, this is the goal of the Germans: 'The Final Solution.' All prisoners work for the purpose of the crematoria.

"Apart from that, there are two German factories in Auschwitz, Krupp and Siemens, and ten kilometers away in the Buna camp, there is another factory producing synthetic rubber. They use us prisoners as the labor force in all these factories and in others as well.

"Today, tomorrow, they will divide you into groups. The groups are called *Kommandos* and each of you will be assigned to work in a *Kommando*. If you want to extend your life, even for a short while, you must work. Whoever does not work is burned here. Believe us, we older prisoners unfortunately know the whole operation of the camp. There are prisoners here who have survived for more than four years under these conditions. The first to come here long before we did were German Jews and Jews from Czechoslovakia. They went through hell, almost all died. Burned. Of them all, very few women are still alive in our camp and those few became *Kapos*, our supervisors. They pretend to obey the Germans because they don't want to die, and they have many privileges — they don't suffer any longer from hunger."

God, how did they endure so many years.... What kept them going? What we were hearing was very harsh, unacceptable. Something absurd is happening here, I see. It is really a very well thought-out hell — a hell that you live, you see, you feel ... it's unbelievable! Can it be all our people were burned in this inhumane way? Nobody survived of all those who were on the trucks? All became flames, ashes from yesterday to today? I began losing my mind. I was overcome by fear in the face of all this horror surrounding us!

The injustice, the disgust, the despair threw me from one state to another, until finally into complete apathy. For a moment I didn't even want my own life anymore. For what? Why?

For some time, I wouldn't listen to anything or look at anything. I wasn't interested in this world — a brutal, evil world that burned you. It was an enormous shock. The first shock from which I couldn't recover. From that moment, the abyss of the human soul opened up before me, revealing man completely naked as, it seems, he is by nature — a mixture of good and evil.

Marching to music

The bell at four-thirty in the morning accompanied by the whips of the Polish women mercilessly beating our bodies was our daily *réveille*. It was an inevitable, invariable program. That's how they woke us up for *Appell*.

After roll call outside with its usual procedures, they distributed a breakfast of steamy, thin, watery black coffee in an old rusty cup of military issue from which five of us women drank by turns. It was rumored that they put something in the coffee to stop our periods. In the noon soup, they added something for both men and women prisoners to check our sexual impulses.

And while the gas chambers worked continuously, spitting flames and smoke, the *"Kommando Orchester"* was ordered to play Mozart or military marches. Prisoners who were virtuosi coming from the great cities of Europe and Russia had brought their Stradivarius and Amati violins with them on their "journey of deception."

All our feet had to march to the rhythm of the music while our hands, on the contrary, had to remain immobile, nailed against our body. In this way, all *Kommandos*, without exception, went off for work to musical accompaniment.

Our group was called *Aussenkommando*. Accompanied by the *Kapos* and by SS holding hounds, we started marching to the sound of music, five-five to a row on a muddy road full of puddles from the rain. We walked very far before finally arriving at our destination.

It really was a stony area as the older prisoners had told us. As soon as we stopped, we realized how difficult things were going to be. We were forced to labor and ordered to lift huge heavy stones, carry them a mile further away, only to bring them back to the very same place we had found them.

The SS would laugh and enjoy our hardships. Woe to whomever did not work actively and quickly. The dogs were trained to attack prisoners and on command jump and bite pitilessly. At times the dogs were ordered to finish off their victims as an example to others.

The load of stone I was carrying was heavy. My delicate hands could not bear it anymore. I was shaking from despair and indignation and ready to fall ... when, as in a dream, I heard someone calling me from afar! I hardly heard my name I was so absorbed and immersed in my gloomy thoughts. It was my friend Dora, drawing me out of my stupor and trying to save me once again.

"Berry, Berry, hold on. Keep your morale high. Don't yield. One day we must get out of this place alive."

Despite trusting her a lot, at that moment ... right then, I could no longer understand her. Dora was unrealistic!

"How can you reconcile yourself to this terrible situation? How can you live without hope at this primitive level? How can we escape this deadly hell?"

"With *will* power. If our will is strong, we are even able to cut the charged barbed wires ... like that, as if we held a magic pair of scissors in our hands (and she motioned with her hands). Such is the power man possesses if he wishes."

I looked at her with wide-open eyes, astounded. She was not debilitated like me. Dora was still holding on. Where does she draw this strength from, I wondered.... Could I possibly have some strength inside me as well? Could I make an effort after all? With death encircling us, can I somehow keep it at bay for a while?

On the other hand, does it really matter? How much longer are we going to live? First we must acknowledge our situation. Life is the here and now. There is no future. But perhaps time will lead to more time ... who knows?

My silent despair and Dora's shouting, stimulated my imagination. Diffidently, I whispered to myself: Yes, the Latins said a long time ago, "Woe to the losers." Thus, at that moment a new goal was born: death didn't matter to me anymore, but as long as I was alive, I would not let myself down.

Suddenly, I recall, I felt an enormous current arising from my very depths. It was that powerful awakening called "the survival instinct." They say we carry it within us from the moment we are born and that it comes forward only at the right moment to prevent us from dying.

Then, I recall, my "astral body" became heavy like iron and completely covered me. An outer shield suddenly formed around me. This shield no longer let any arrow penetrate my shell. It meant that bad

A Cry for Tomorrow 76859 ...

news and unpleasant messages from outside stopped there — didn't touch me. Apparently, a defense mechanism automatically created itself inside me, protecting me, postponing feelings for a later time.

Without realizing it I made an extraordinary decision: For the time being I forbade myself to have any strong emotions. No tears, I said, or powerful feelings. I must conserve my energy and strength, at least for now. It was self-assertion or self-defense. At the time, I couldn't say — but I wanted to survive.

Upon returning to camp Birkenau, the marching band was waiting for us at the gate: *Eins-zwei-drei, eins-zwei* ... "One-two-three, one-two...."

At seven o'clock at night, *Appell* again. And at nine o'clock, before going to bed — punishment!

Two of my first cousins, Regina and her older sister, and two or three of our fellow citizens had their honorary treatment that night. Kneeling on the frozen floor with their hands held high, they had to remain in that position for half-an-hour. In front of them the Polish women with the whips watched in case they moved.

I watched without emotion; didn't move from my place; and when their punishment finally ended, I remember, I went and stood by their side speechless, looking at them. I didn't know what to say. I didn't speak.

The days went by, each one more intolerable than the last, and at night we fell into bed physically and mentally exhausted from the hardships of the day.

One night, which I will never forget, two familiar voices woke us up. A mother and her daughter (recent arrivals) were screaming and pulling each other's hair in the dark. (They both survived and I ask permission not to mention their names.)

Beside herself with crying and shouting, the daughter had fallen on her mother and was shaking her: "Oh mother, it was you," she said, "it was you who stole the little piece of bread I kept under my head for tomorrow? You were the last person I expected to do such a thing! How could you? How could you steal from your own flesh and blood?"

In a frenzy the mother replied, "I'm hungry! I want to live too. What mother will give birth to me again?"

I was astounded! Where are we? I asked myself. In this place, people will gradually lose every vestige of conscience to save their skin for just one more day.

Indeed, the Germans were counting on just that: to completely dehumanize us and turn us into beasts. But it remains for us to choose and decide, I said to myself. We can either face pain and death wretchedly, or with dignity and pride.

Next morning on my way to *Aussenkommando* labor, I happened to be in my row of five next to a newcomer, a young woman from Thessaloniki named Jeanne Shalom.* I was shivering from the cold and my hands, like two pieces of wood, were numb from freezing. I blew into my hands trying to warm them up perhaps, but nothing helped.

"What are you doing?" Jeanne asked me. "Are you Greek?"

"Yes," I replied, "I am Greek, and you?"

"Oh poor girl, your hands, they're shaking from the cold! Come, give them to me. Put them in this glove." And with that she immediately took off one of her gloves. (She possessed them from somewhere.) "They're large gloves, so both hands will fit in," she said. "Take one of mine for yourself to warm up somehow, and I will put both my hands in the other."

Is it possible? I didn't expect such a thing. I stared at her in disbelief! Are there still human beings here, I wondered? That glove that moment was the warmest human caress, for like a flame it warmed and rejoiced my soul and my whole body.

Selektion

One day when I was feeling miserable and very tired, I decided to avoid work no matter what, and remain in the block pretending to be very sick. I had to inform the *Blockoberst*, who would declare number 76859 absent from the *Aussenkommando* due to illness. Of course, I was taking a risk because in these situations they would either send you to a different block, which was supposedly the "clinic" to give you an aspirin, or make you face some other dire consequence.

Daisy looked at me very skeptically, but I was unmoved.

As soon as all *Kommandos* left for work to the accompaniment of music, etc., I went to my straw bunk bed and lay down for a while to rest my tired body. Around ten o'clock in the morning, the SS began visiting the neighboring blocks for "sorting" or *"Selektion"* as they called it there. We saw SS in the camp only during "official" visits, that is to say, to carry out some order or for something strange. Not that there was anything which was not strange inside there.

---

*Jeanne survived and I meet her very often here in Athens, and each time I thank her for that glove. "Do you remember?" I ask her, "I will never forget you or your glove."

A Cry for Tomorrow 76859 ...

The only thing Daisy and her assistant had time to tell me, was to run and disappear, lest they visit our block and take me away for not working.

I was terrified and ran across to a barrack that was used as a toilet. The toilet-barrack had two long wooden boards with many holes for our physical needs. When we entered there, we sometimes saw ten women at a time. It was disgusting. Their bodies, full of pimples and pus, were repulsive, especially those of the older girls! I had no choice and went in there to hide. As I opened the door I saw two girls I did not know, who at that moment were looking through the cracks to see whether the SS were coming to catch them.

They told me a *Selektion* was in progress in their block and they were taking away the sick, the feeble girls, and all those who had pimples. They were to be burned in the crematorium. By sending all the girls with pimples and contagious diseases to the crematoria, the Germans kept the camps clean. Conditions in the camp were so bad that the simplest illness, even the most benign, was dangerous. Every little pimple on dirty, filthy bodies could readily become an incurable wound.

Listening to them in horror, I looked outside for myself and saw many other girls running here and there toward the attics, the toilets, wherever they could — hunted, breathless, weak, bony. The barking of the dogs and the voices of the SS were approaching ever closer and closer.

"Oh God, they'll soon be here," one said, terrified.

The other continued apathetically:

"Do you think we'll escape again today?"

In a daze, I spontaneously started humming some muddled words from a song I just happened to think of. Was I drunk? Of course not, one doesn't get drunk without alcohol and food, but I remember saying these words to myself:

> Don't cry, Spanish woman, don't grieve.
> Everything will turn out as you wish ...
> Don't cry, Spanish woman, don't grieve, etc....

I didn't know what I was singing, but I repeated it over and over. I'm afraid it didn't even sound like a song, but I wanted it to come out of me as music, as a prayer, or as courage against the agony and pain I felt at that moment — that harsh moment of *Selektion* for death!

I continued singing until the barking and the voices could not be heard anymore.... The SS turned and went in another direction to find other girls for the furnaces.

From then on and for as long as I lived in the camp, every time I faced great danger that little song came spontaneously and instinctively to my lips. Apparently it had become my little prayer, or perhaps my lucky charm.

These *Selektionen* were carried out quite often in the Birkenau and Auschwitz camps. And each time the same scenario, the same scenes. General unrest ensued! But each one of us reacted with our own feelings in a different way. One reacted in a revolutionary way; another in a fatalistic way; yet another in a hopeful way, each believing that her own god would save her once more. Others, desperate, unable to play games with death day in and day out, sought the final solution themselves. They committed suicide, throwing themselves on the charged barbed wires which left them dead on the ground immediately.

I experienced these events every moment of every day.

I soon learned everything concerning the camp's operation, in all its facets. Prisoners who had been there for awhile, didn't stop narrating and explaining the whole system in all possible detail. But slowly I saw for myself the hideous reality.

Block 10 – Dr. Mengele

The "Angel of Death" of Auschwitz — this is what they called Mengele in the camp. He carried out experiments in Block 10 and his guinea pigs were prisoners. He had a great interest in twins, and as soon as he heard that "transports" were about to arrive at the railway station, he joyfully ran to make the *Selektionen* himself, to find the living material on which he would then try whatever his satanic mind could think of. On men, he would remove one testicle, sometimes both. On women, he would perform a variety of experiments, including inserting sperm of monkeys into their ovaries and wait for the results he could later contribute to "science."

In Block 10, he himself was the one who literally cut and sewed without first administering any anesthesia, indifferent to the pain and suffering of the prisoners. For Mengele it did not matter if the "subhumans" died under his scalpel. He had plenty of people at his disposal and could replace them instantly.

All men and women who found themselves in Block 10 were deceptively given some temporary nourishment at first. But then, after they became human rags in his hands, they were often sent back to the labor blocks to work for as long as they would last. Thus, these unfortunate creatures would come to us and tell us in their own words what had happened, showing us their sewed-up bellies. These poor souls were still aching from having one or both of their ovaries removed.

Mengele's goal was to find a quick method of sterilization that could be used for mass biological extermination of whole nations, especially Jews, Poles, Czechs, and Russians. Dr. Carl Clauberg of Königsberg, who was also involved in these experiments, wrote the following in one of the letters he sent to Himmler: "We have almost laid hands on the method. We are in a position to sterilize up to one thousand individuals per day." (From the Auschwitz Museum archives.)

Other kinds of experiments were also carried out in Block 10. At the request of the Consortium, German corporations — the large firm "Bayer" for example — sent various drugs to the camp to be tested on prisoners. Conclusions were then drawn in relation to the effects these chemical products had on the human organism.

The "Hospital"

In the barrack where we slept, we had two sisters from Thessaloniki — Germaine and Claire.* Both enjoyed some protection and support from Daisy, the *Blockoberst*. They owed this to a friend of Daisy called Marina Halegua who was Germaine's former seamstress in Thessaloniki, and who was also a prisoner in our block.

One day they asked for two women from our block who knew how to knit, to be sent to the *Revier*, or "hospital," for fifteen to twenty

---

*Germaine and her sister Claire survived and live in Athens. They both lost their husbands in the camps, but both women were reunited with their daughters. Germaine was reunited with her three daughters and Claire with her only daughter. The reverent nuns of the French School had hidden them throughout the German occupation.

The number on Germaine's arm is A 8313.

The Polish midwife, Stanislava, assisted 3,000 women in childbirth and 3,000 times obeyed the inhumane orders of the Nazi executioner who decided that: all new born babies be immediately drowned in a slop-pail with its excrement.

In the camp, the midwife was assigned number 41336 and her daughter number 41337. (They were not Jews, but were arrested by the Gestapo in the years of Nazi occupation because she and her husband were supplying food, clothes, and identity cards to Jews.)

Mother and daughter remained together the entire time. Her daughter Sylvia is one of the few eye witnesses of the Auschwitz atrocity.

days. Naturally, conditions would be better there than in the *Aussenkommando*. Marina Halegua persuaded her friend Daisy to send both sisters there.

This was a secret agreement for Germaine and Claire. There, of course, they would eat better, but they had to knit various things for a certain officer of the SS named Dr. Shultze, who lived with his family on the other side of the camp. (Many SS officers lived with their families in princely conditions, of course, just opposite us outside the camp.) Well, the officer's wife sent wool to the *Revier* and ordered various clothes to be made for herself and her children. As long as the sisters knitted, they were under the protection of a higher official and not threatened with *Selektionen*.

The *Revier* was an extension of Block 10. It was the hospital used for convalescence. Girls who suffered from some epidemic or illness were sent there for alleged treatment. It was also said that the *Revier* was a waiting room for the crematoria.

When the girls who knitted were not needed anymore (it seems the Germans were afraid to keep them too long) they sent them back to the block where we slept.

I remember when Germaine came back to us. She was terrified because she could not get over what she had seen there. Both sisters lived through the most horrible experiences. She said that except for the nurses, the *Kapos* and the doctors, most prisoners were so sick that they lacked the strength to move from their bunk beds. Others feebly wandered in the corridors with high fever or diarrhea.

Germaine said one day she lived through something so horrible that she would never forget it as long as she lived. A sick woman, a member of the Rothschild family, was so ill with high fever that the poor thing defecated on herself. Her diarrhea was so bad that she also soiled the floor. As soon as the *Kapo* arrived and saw the situation, she lost her temper and angrily ordered the woman to fall on her knees and lick up her excrement with her tongue. The *Kapo's* whip ordered and threatened. She was not kidding! The unfortunate Rothschild had no other choice but to obey.

Germaine experienced even worse events than these. Pregnant women arriving in Auschwitz for the first *Selektion* often did not declare their pregnancy (some being only days or months pregnant and not yet aware of it). These hapless women waited to give birth in *Revier* or were the victims of experiments. After giving birth, Germaine told us, the newborn babies were immediately taken and in front of their mothers'

A Cry for Tomorrow 76859 ...

eyes, submerged head first in boiling water or drowned in the slop pail of excrement. This brutal, cruel process went on almost every day.

Diary of the Auschwitz midwife*

Sylvia wrote:
   In the so-called 'hospital' of the camp, when the German Clara, a professional midwife and killer of the babies born there, fell ill, my mother found the courage to present herself before the SS doctor and show him her professional card as a midwife. She had managed to hide this card when they took all our things away. Perhaps her courage and her sudden action saved her from death. Mengele thought of something... and kept her in the 'hospital' appointing her midwife.

*Stanislava Lesinska** wrote in her short diary:*
   In the barrack on the right and left sides, were four-storied wooden beds, and there, on dirty rags stained with dry blood and excrement, two or three women lay in each bed. In the middle of the corridor there was a table-top stove that heated from both sides. There the women gave birth to their babies. There was no other source of heat in the barrack. The bitter cold pierced the bones and icicles hung from the ceiling.

Sylvia wrote:
   After a few days they called my mother to go and see the doctor of the camp. Mengele ordered her to kill all babies as soon as they were born.

Stanislava continued:
   Until May 1943, all babies born in the camp were killed in the most horrible way. They drowned them in the barrel containing the excrement, in the so-called 'slop pail'. The German woman Clara, an ex-nurse convicted of infanticide, had undertaken their extermination.
   We could hear the sound of the bubbles when she drowned

---

*Quoted from the article of M. Ap. Kotsiolis, published in the newspaper "Ta Nea" on 9.10.1983.

**Stanislava Lesinska died on March 11, 1974. Thousands accompanied her to her grave surrounded by a sea of flowers, among whom were Leukandia Neviadomski, number 87945 of Auschwitz, and her son, born in Stanislava's hands.

the babies. The next day the unfortunate mother would see the little body of her child outside the barrack, eaten by mice.

The "Auschwitz Midwife," Stanislava, finished her diary with the following words:

I am writing this, speaking on behalf of all those who did not live to tell the world the ordeal they went through. Through my mouth, the mothers and the babies of Auschwitz are speaking.

In Auschwitz there were four women's camps and in these camps, 150 *Kommando* groups. There were also two munitions factories, Union and Dan, manufacturing explosives, boxes for bombshells and wooden products. Many girls worked in the Union factory and they were pleased, poor women, because they had a roof over their head instead of being outside with the stones in the mud.

Every *Kommando* was the microcosm of a human society, a multiform little world. There, Jews from every corner of Europe, along with Gypsies, Germans, criminals, political activists, Soviet partisans, Polish anti-nazis, Armenians, and others, were obliged to co-exist.

Everybody there had been charged with a "crime": political, religious or racial. These masses of people of such great variety were obliged to work under the worst living conditions of the totalitarian Hitlerite regime, mainly for the extermination of others and finally for their own extermination. The prisoners themselves built the roads leading to their own hell. They themselves built the barracks and the blocks. They themselves built Block 11, "The Bunker," and the well-known crematoria.

Block 11

Block 11 was called the "Block of Death." In the basement of Block 11 there were small cellars, ninety centimeters long by ninety centimeters wide, and others much larger to hold many people. They threw prisoners destined for punishment or condemned to death into these cellars. These victims received almost no food and very rarely did anyone get out alive. High walls surrounded the yard of the block. Under these walls 20,000 prisoners were shot in the head and back. Then their bodies were thrown into wood fires or into large trenches and burned.

In 1941, when a train arrived with 600 Soviet prisoners destined for mass execution, they decided to close all of them in the cellars of Block 11 and kill them using a gas called "Zyklon B." Zyklon B was a deadly powder used in the camp initially for disinfection. This test had the result they aimed for. Still, death was slow. Later, in another test, they found the appropriate dose, able to kill a large mass of people in a few minutes.

Rudolf Hoess, in charge of preparing the extermination of the Jews in his camp, thought he could successfully use the discovery of Zyklon B to carry out the task of mass executions. In one of Eichmann's visits to Auschwitz, Hoess informed him of his plans, and they agreed together to proceed quickly with the "Final Solution" of the Jews.

> *"Neither the higher quantity of alcohol, nor the absence of witnesses when only the two of them were present, ever changed Eichmann's fixed idea of destroying every Jew who would fall into his hands."*
>
> From the biography of the Commander of Auschwitz, Rudolf Hoess

The crematoria

The firm *Topf und Söhne* of Erfurt, quickly built four gas chambers in Birkenau and Auschwitz, using the most up to date techniques. (The foundry's trademark can still be seen on various pieces of metal that have been preserved.)

The crematoria were three storied. First they led the victims into the basement, a closed space which looked like a shower room. Many showerheads had even been placed in the ceiling to deceive the prisoners. There, the prisoners stripped naked, and before the victims could put up any resistance, they were kicked and beaten into the next hall that connected with the previous one through a heavy metal door. They were squeezed in, one on top of the other, until the hall was jam-packed. After the door was hermetically closed, the SS threw Zyklon B into the room through a special little window they would open, high above. Small blue pellets dropped from a box exploded into gas, causing certain death.

When the iron door was opened fifteen to twenty minutes later, the dead fell like pieces of wood. Then came the turn of the *Sonderkommando*. This was a specially chosen group of Jews forced to work in the crematoria. Once they were working inside, they had no contact with the rest of the prisoners. They were isolated. These unfortunate people were obliged to take the corpses out of the gas chambers and remove all the valuables they had on them, such as gold teeth, watches, rings, earrings, etc. (The human hair was sold and used for bombsites and mattresses.)

Then they sent the bodies by elevator to the furnaces on the upper floor. There the bodies were burned. The body fat was made into the soap that we prisoners used for washing. The ashes were thrown into various little lakes around the region.

Sonderkommandos performed this hard work for only two or three months, sometimes a little longer. Then they themselves — the silent grave-diggers of their own race — had to be burned after a while, as they could not last longer. This was the system.

In the beginning, 2,000 corpses were burned in the crematoria daily, but soon production reached 10,000 and at a certain point it rose to 25,000 per day. Thus, from 1941 to 1945, 1,600,000 people disappeared in the Auschwitz crematoria. A "factory of death" was the way, and correctly so, Kulka, an ex-Jewish prisoner of the Germans, expressed it in his book, to tell us that:

> Zyklon B was produced by the German firm Deutsche Gesellschaft zur Schädlingsbekämpfung Degesch and the company, Tech. Stabenau, was in charge of its supply. In the period 1941-1944, IG-Farbenindustria, that belonged to the Degesch company, earned 300,000 Marks from the gas it sold.

Testimonies by Greek *Sonderkommandos*

Danny Bennahmias

I quote here an interview sent by a good friend of mine. He was a co-prisoner and in this interview he speaks of the rare experience he went through in the Crematorium. His name was Danny Bennahmias. He owned an optical company after working for twenty-three years as a chemist. He lived in Oakland, California, where he died, and both his children are graduates of the University of California, Berkeley.

Testimony of Bennahmias:

Before the war, I was an only child born in Thessaloniki. At the age of eighteen, I was deported by the Germans to Auschwitz with my parents.... Unfortunately, my father and mother were selected to be burned in the crematorium. I was destined by fate to work in *Sonderkommando* inside the crematorium — that is to say, in the gas chambers.

Prisoners, sick and emaciated because of hunger, were

brought to us, and they were obliged to take off their clothes in order to allegedly take a bath. Afterwards, like a flock, they were led into a huge room where they were hermetically closed inside. Then SS soldiers threw the gas from above, to asphyxiate them.

My job, Bennahmias says, was to untangle the human corpses. As they died, they became entangled one upon the other, no doubt from the agony of asphyxiation. Then, when they were finally dead, we had to separate the tangled corpses one by one. After that process, another group, similar to mine, took them to burn them in the furnaces.

In Crematorium IV there was a quite large furnace, deep and wide, able to burn 6,000 human corpses daily.

The first night on this job, I fainted five times. Luckily, two Poles who were near me and did the same job, stood me up each time, shouting at me to bring me back to my senses, for had the Germans seen me in this state, they would have shot me on the spot.

Once for one week only, I went out and did another job, but then they took me back again in the *Sonderkommando*.

After some time, I apparently overcame the shock, and from then on I was able to work ... without food and warm clothes, the two basic things a man needs to go on living. In this situation, one loses his strength and does not know how to respond.

But despite all this, myself with several others in 1944 tried to revolt against our torturers. We conceived a plan to seize the soldiers' arms and free ourselves, but the signal for the revolt went wrong. Many prisoners went out, believing they were free and the guards killed them all. German officers, who arrived with trucks and police hounds, found me and my friends ... but the dead were so many, that they kept us alive in order to collect and burn the corpses.

As the Russians were approaching, they tried to exterminate all of us as soon as possible because they didn't want to leave witnesses and evidence behind. They appointed a group of fifteen to take care of our execution, but the Russian troops were about to arrive at any moment so they quickly stacked us in an open train and sent us to Mauthausen, and from there to Austria, to another death camp called "Ebensee."

We stayed there until May 8, the date of our liberation by General Patton. Only fifteen to twenty people survived from my group, which consisted of 1,000 men.

AUSCHWITZ

It was a miracle I was saved. My feet were swollen and I could not walk. When I finally recovered, I went to Athens to start my life anew. I married and came to America with my family.*

MARCEL NADJARI

Marcel Nadjari was one of the few Greeks from Thessaloniki who survived the *Sonderkommando*. When he returned to Greece, he was called up as a soldier and almost nightly during his military service, he wrote down the horrible experiences he went through in the *Sonderkommando*.

Married with two children, he later moved to America. On many of my trips to New York, I visited him. We often recalled incidents from the days we were both prisoners in Auschwitz. Unfortunately, Marcel died relatively young about twenty years ago.

Yet now, I quote in my book from one part of his memoirs, which his wife Rosa and his lovely daughter Nelly so generously handed over to me. I thank them both very much, because for me it is very important to complement my book with documents coming from other witnesses who experienced the same nightmare.

Testimony of Marcel Nadjari:

The German commander summoned us and told us that we would leave the quarantine block on the following day to work in a nice place. Much work, he said, but much food as well. We were all joyful. They gathered 150 and put us in Block 13 from which nobody could get out alive. Block 13 was the *Sonderkommando*. As we entered, we were received by the older prisoners (who had been there before us): Poles, Polish-French, and a Frenchman named Michel, whose parents were from Thessaloniki.

My mind could not grasp what we were going to do. Looking at the older ones staring at us, I felt a flicker of fear, as if something very evil was in store for me.

The group received us very well and the first thing they did

---

*Danny Bennahmias donated the prison uniform that he wore in the camp until the time of his liberation to the Athens Jewish Museum.

For the full story of Daniel Bennahmias' experiences as a *Sonderkommando* see *The Holocaust Odyssey of Daniel Bennahmias, Sonderkommando*, by Rebecca Camhi Fromer, The University of Alabama Press, Tuscaloosa, Alabama, 1993.

was to give us as much food as we could eat: bread, jam, and various sweets, not camp food. In the beginning, we didn't ask where it came from, nor were we interested to learn. Just being able to eat was the height of happiness. Then I struck up a conversation with the Poles, who were good people, and with someone who was sick, with whom we later became very good friends. From the few things they told me, I understood what hell we had entered into.

The beds were the same as those of the quarantine block. The person in charge of 13 was the worst man imaginable. A Pole from France, huge, always ironic. Once I received four slaps in the face of rare severity. He nearly beat us to death; kicking, beating, punching, and slapping were a daily routine.

They divided us into four groups, I, II, III, and the Forest group. The men of group I would go to Crematorium I, which was large. Those of group II to Crematorium II, also large, and group III to Crematorium IV, which was small. The fourth group went outside the camp to the so-called "Bunker 11," where they dug trenches and gathered dry branches — the worst job of all.

They took us to Crematorium I. I had with me Vico, Brudo, Moise, Aaron, and others. First they put us to work in the yard, to level out the ground in one corner. Later, in our room, we were prohibited from going out. We were nervous, and looked through the window to see what was going on outside. Suddenly we saw trucks arriving full of women, children, elderly women, the lame, young mothers, pregnant women.

They got everyone down from the trucks, and then guided them down a stairway to a hall in the basement. The trucks left immediately to be loaded with more people and come back. About thirty to thirty-five trucks arrived, fully loaded.

Then there was silence.

After about an hour we went out into the yard again to do the same work. Suddenly the *Kapo* gathered us together again. He was good to us Greeks and got on well with the Germans, especially with *Oberscharführer* Muhsfeld, head of both crematoria I and II — an evil man, a sadist of the highest degree. They took us down a stairway to a hall in the basement where only shortly before the women and the men had entered. They ordered us to take off the old, tattered clothes we were wearing and choose whatever clothes we liked that were there. The hall looked like a sea of clothes. None of us wanted to touch them. But after being beaten with sticks and intimidated by force, I took a brown jacket that I kept throughout the time I spent in the *Sonder*. There in the corridor of the *Auskleideraum,* the "disrobing room," where we were and where the people we had just seen with our own eyes shortly before had undressed, was an open door, and exactly at the threshold of that door we saw a mass of corpses.

Our fear was enormous. We ran across the corridor and began ascending the stairs, terrified. Each one told the other what we had seen. They took us by there at least daily to get us used to that scene. I remained at Crematorium II, while Moise, Aaron, Vico, Brudo, and Isaac Baruch went to Crematorium IV. I begged them to stay with me, so that we might die together when the hour came, but in vain. They said it was better to be scattered, in case one of us got out alive and able to tell everything to others.

Chief over all the crematoria was Moll, a short, blond man whose tic closed his right eye every other moment. He was a monster ... and to amuse himself, placed old men at a distance of 15 to 20 meters and shot them in various parts of their body: in the eyes, in the ears, in the penis, anywhere, and then threw them into the trench. He was the terror of the camp and even of Kramer himself.*

Moll, being an excellent marksman, would put women at some distance and shoot them in their breasts. Once he dumped a whole truckload of the sick into a trench and burned them alive, where they died in atrocious pain. He was unique in the world: not a man, nor an animal, but a monster ... who didn't keep a whip in his hand, only a revolver. So differences were swiftly resolved.

One day, an order came for all the Greeks to work at Bunker 11 by the trenches. In charge were Moll and the *Kapo*. It was our darkest night. That evening they brought approximately 4,000 Hungarian Jews to the bunker. After poisoning them, group after

---

*Josef Kramer, in charge of the gas chambers and crematoria in Auschwitz II - Birkenau, loved music very much and would often go to hear the camp orchestra play Schumann and Bach. Despite this fact, he never shied away from participating in that characteristic SS group frenzy when they would load the wagons for the crematorium. He set the example, becoming far more savage than the others ... and never hesitated smashing the head of some woman or small child by beating them with his club.

group, they threw them through the back door into the trenches.

We Greeks usually had the task of taking corpses out of the gas chamber and pulling them over to the trenches, where four others grabbed them and with a "one, two, three," threw them into the trenches. The heat from the fire (lit to incinerate them) was unbearable. The flames, the rain, the killing of so many thousands of women and children, the beatings by the *Vorarbeiter* or *Kapo*, and the shootings by Moll, made us start losing sense of what we were doing.

Moll shot the first of us when Moll ordered him to do something he didn't understand. Another one of us, not being able to endure any longer, was thrown into the fire alive. *Oberscharführer* Staimberg went over to end the suffering, and shot at him until his screams were not heard anymore.

That night we had all decided to die, but the thought of revenge and the desire to organize an escape kept us alive. Then German orders separated us into four groups: 100 at Crematorium I, 100 at Crematorium II, 400 (approx.) at Crematorium IV, 600 (approx.) at the Bunker and 11 at the trenches.

I was at Crematorium II. We were thirty-five Greeks in all and were able to communicate between I and II.

All crematoria worked uninterruptedly. Hungarians came from Hungarian towns of the Carpathians near Romania. Each day two or three trains arrived and each train had 2,500 to 3,000 persons. At Crematoria I and II, the order was to burn to ashes 2,500 people every twenty-four hours. Our crematorium consisted first of a huge room, the *Auskleideraum*, that is to say, the "disrobing room," and second of the *Gasraum*, a room of the same dimensions. As soon as they stepped down from the trains, and after the *Selektion*, the Germans escorted them to us. There were signs posted along their way and all had the impression they were going to a disinfection station and bath house.

Most had a smile on their faces and even their gestures gave us courage. When they arrived at our entrance, they would then go down the stairs to the *Auskleideraum*. There we received them. First we told them to sit and rest for a bit, if a German wasn't looking of course. Then the Germans shouted *ausziehen*, meaning "undress", and we also told them to do so.

The young girls felt shy and found it difficult to undress, and would cry from embarrassment — not because they would be dead a few minutes later, as this they did not know.

Others though gave us gold coins and told us to keep them. We took them despite the fact we had no need for them, we just wanted to prevent the Germans from taking them, who watched like hawks. Others, more perceptive and alert, came and asked us whether they were about to be killed. I always answered that I didn't understand German, or any other language apart from Greek. But, believe it or not, once an old man, whom I told I didn't know any other language except Greek, started talking to me in ancient Greek. He was a professor at the University of Hungary.

The heartbreak of watching little children cry because they had the presentiment of death, caused us sorrow. We tried to approach them, but they were afraid of us, as if we were the messengers of their death. On the other hand, others showed us love. For laughs, the Germans told them to take soap with them and ordered them to tie their shoes together (*Schuhe zusammenbinden*) and hold them in their hands.

Most of the people thought they were going to take a bath, since "Disinfection Room" was written on the corridor door in German, French, Hungarian, Czech, and English. When the door opened, each woman tried to get in first to take a good position for her bath. Once inside, they gathered and waited for the room to fill. In the meantime, the men stepped down into the changing room and wondered how they would possibly get their clothes back, since everything was jumbled up in a huge sea.

The exact procedure was repeated, for they also entered the gas chamber. Then, after everybody had been squeezed in, the door was closed. Immediately, two gas specialists went up, opened four canisters and emptied them from above while laughing or discussing trivialities. Then they replaced the concrete plate.

Peering through the small window in the door, a chronometer in hand, they would often observe how many minutes it would take for everyone to die. (It took six to seven minutes.)

From the moment the door was firmly shut and the first quantity of gas fell from above, everybody understood they were going to die and started moving toward the small door, stepping over one another. Those who fell down always died faster from asphyxiation, especially the disabled or the small children who

A Cry for Tomorrow 76859 ...

became separated from their mothers. People tried to save themselves ... scratching at the walls with their nails.

The door was completely covered with nail scratches. During the few minutes before they died, they apparently suffered greatly. The Germans watched through the aperture and laughed....

From outside we could hear their banging and the biblical Hebrew prayer, the *Shemah*, which they recited. Even at the end, they were always waiting for a miracle.

After completing their mission, the specialists who threw the gas got into their car again (a health department vehicle with huge red crosses and a small Red Cross flag) and left.

Then our work began. We had to collect the clothing of the dead and take it out to the trucks for transport to Kanada for sorting (Kanada was another *Kommando*). In the meantime, we searched all pockets for valuables under the noses of the Germans.

We found dollars, gold, small purses ... anything one could imagine. We managed to hide most everything, giving up only things of little value to them who, in turn, kept it all for themselves, hiding it from their superiors. For us, gold, dollars, and precious gems did not mean much, but for the German soldiers, it meant everything. Often times they became our pawns, and would do us all kinds of favors, provided we paid them.

Afterward, we would spread open a coat or raincoat, fill it with clothes, tie the sleeves, load them on our backs, climb up the small ladder, and throw them into the trucks.

About an hour after the death of those people, special ventilation machines ("Electrician Sam") sucked out the poisonous air. With the opening of the door, we heard nothing but the noise of the bodies jammed around the door falling heavily on the concrete floor .

Then a frightening silence reigned. People who shortly before had been screaming and shouting, were now silent, as if they had fallen asleep. I myself doubted whether these were the same people with whom I had spoken a short while before, people whose faces full of fear and terror were now tranquil, as if they were resting....

Our work consisted of pulling the bodies out with a cane by

the neck. With a belt wrapped around our hand, we pulled them to the elevator. When it was filled with six or seven corpses, we knocked twice with the cane. The elevator would suddenly move to the upper floor, three meters above, where another group — mostly Greeks — received the freight and shoved it into the mouth of the furnace, three at a time.

Before stacking them into the elevator, a barber moved along with a pair of scissors cutting off the women's hair which was put into a sack and delivered to Crematorium I, where it was dried and then delivered to another service for unknown use. It was rumored that the hair was fabricated into soles for shoes, seat cushions, or more likely, pillows for air force pilots.

The children were thrown pell-mell into the furnace. When corpses were stacked in front of the furnace, about forty-five at a time, *der Zahnarzt*, "the dentist," Leon Cohen, would pass by with a pincer to examine all mouths. Wherever he found a golden, bronze or white — metal tooth or denture, he pulled them out and put them into a case. The furnaces operated for thirty minutes. One out of every three corpses had to be a female, because that made cremation faster. About every six hours the ashes were emptied into pushcarts and thrown into the trenches. When some people were brought for execution, they were shot in the neck and their corpses were also taken to the furnaces — those insatiable mouths.

This tortured life of mine lasted eight and one-half months. From moment to moment we waited for our deliverance: death. The only thing that kept us alive was our desire for revenge and the organized attempt to escape that we unanimously planned with the Russians.

Here is the plan we had in mind ever since our first days in *Sonderkommando:* Paying a handsome sum in dollars, we acquired dynamite from the Union factory, transported it in the little wagon that carried soup every day to all *Kommandos,* and buried it in the courtyard of the crematorium.

Each crematorium had three Germans armed with rifles and pistols. We planned to attack them and obtain our first six guns. Then, every night at exactly six o'clock the night shift arrived, about twenty-five Germans armed with automatic weapons and double-barreled shotguns.

They marched by in columns of five and at the precise

moment when they would be at the entrance of the courtyard, we would all attack them with whatever we could find and then divvy up their guns. Then we would go to the neighboring *Lagers* or "camps" and free the others.

The job was indeed delicate, but we were determined no matter what. The plan was exactly the same for Crematoria III and IV.

We set the date, but unfortunately at noon on the day the operation was to take place, it was postponed because a train full of Poles arrived between Crematoria I and II. The day after, Kamitsky (our *Kapo*) was arrested. They killed him in Crematorium IV together with Gypsies. Fortunately, he didn't utter a word concerning what we were planning against them. He rose to the occasion in his last moments.

But his arrest meant the end of our plans. We knew someone among us had betrayed us. We never learned who it was.

Meanwhile, the first amongst us suffered *Selektion* for cremation. They took the first two hundred, including Yakoel, the lawyer Faratzis, and Markesis Levy with whom we had become good friends. They gassed them in Auschwitz in the disinfection room and brought the corpses back to us. The Germans themselves burned them.

The more time passed, the more we saw our end approaching. Now even the transports where scanty. Another two hundred suffered *Selektion* among those who worked in *Sonderkommando* including Vico, Moise, Aaron, and Zak Baruch. But at three o'clock we saw Crematorium III enveloped in flames and heard shots. The *Kommandoführer* and a man called Post left, and the place filled with SS. Soon they ordered everybody to go downstairs. We Greeks were resigned to set the place on fire and be burned inside the crematorium.

The Poles, especially Orer and Strassvogel, insisted we do nothing, as it would be futile....

We gave in because most of the men could not agree. We went down and they put another one hundred in the two adjacent rooms for our dead.

Events developed as follows:

The Germans arrived at Crematorium III with the list of the two hundred. First they called one hundred Hungarians whom they sent to the bath of the Gypsy *Lager*. Then they called another one hundred to whom they gave half a piece of bread and cheese.

As they started calling the Greeks, the latter did not answer and suddenly a Greek rushed out and shouted: "The Dan, yes or no!" (It was the signal for the revolt.)

We all attacked the three Germans immediately — wounding them, no doubt killing one. But instead of dashing out of the crematorium yard, the prisoners gathered inside it.

Meanwhile, the Germans having been alerted, arrived in trucks and the slaughter began. Then confusion ensued.... Those inside the crematorium set it on fire, but because of the smoke they had to get out. The Germans outside slaughtered them. The rest surrendered, including Vico, Moise, and Zak.

The Germans stripped and killed ten at a time, so they wouldn't take up much space.

Crematorium I, seeing the fire, thought the Germans had given the signal to kill us, so they decided to make an exodus. Even though the yard was surrounded by Germans, they left two inside to set off the dynamite. One of them was Michel, a Frenchman ... and somebody else. But at the last minute they lost their courage and the explosion did not take place.

All those who came out of Crematorium I were killed, but all of them - be it only for a few moments — felt free. Among them was Sam Karasso. Zak and many others who acted as real heroes, all chose to die outside, rather than die inside the room a little later.

We burned them ourselves the following day. I myself went with a group and collected them. Zak had fallen near the water tanks. Though the SS had searched the bodies, there were many photographs that I collected, but later lost.

Records of the *Sonder:* 200 people were left, among them only twenty-six Greeks.

The Poles who worked in Crematorium IV behaved worst of all. They could have helped us more with our plans and at the same time warn us because they had ways to do it. But they preferred to go on with their macabre work and die, be it a later hour. Indeed, their life was not to last much longer.

Right there on the spot, we tried to tell the girls everything, explaining to them the whole operation of the crematoria because we were sure that we who had worked in the *Sonderkommando* were not going to live. They would kill us before being liberated, because our eyes had seen more than they should.

The Germans began to hurry. First we blew up all the rooms made of concrete. The work proceeded systematically and quickly. The girls didn't appear anymore. After about January 15, 1945, they did not take us out of the *Lager*.

It felt like something was about to happen. "The Russians are approaching," we were told. Indeed, at night we heard cannon fire from time to time. The hour of freedom was approaching for Auschwitz, and for our end as well.

January 18, 1945, Birkenau was evacuated.

In the general confusion we were mixed in with other prisoners being sent by transport to Germany, during which we suffered another long odyssey. We arrived at Mauthausen, where after much pain and torment, it took us another three to four months before we were definitely free to finally return to Greece.

Malla did not escape

One day coming back from our work, weary as usual from our toil, they took us instead directly to *Lager* Square to witness a hanging – as a warning to obey and comply with orders. (*Lager* was what we called the camp.) It was to be Malla, a nineteen year old Belgian girl, who daringly tried to escape, but, poor thing, did not succeed.

Malla spoke French, German, and Polish and because of her knowledge, the Germans trusted her with the position of chief interpreter. She ingratiated herself with the prisoners who loved and respected her. Malla had fallen in love with Edek, a good-looking Jewish boy who was a member of the Polish resistance. They were able to meet because both occupied high positions. (He was a management secretary.) So one day, they decided to escape together with the help of German and Romanian SS, who were bribed with gold. They provided Edek with an SS uniform; false papers; a revolver for his belt; and male clothes for Malla.

It is believed they walked five kilometers. Malla carried a washbasin on her head accompanied by the supposed "German" Edek. They reached Kozy, a neighboring Polish village. A Polish friend of theirs led them somewhere for the night. The following day, however, the police caught Malla, and having verified her identity, arrested her. Soon after, Edek surrendered.

Now a shocking scene was unfolding in the middle of the

square where all the *Kommandos* were gathered, waiting in horror and agony.*

Malla, accompanied by hangmen, entered the square with her head erect like a heroine, loudly and fearlessly insulting Hitler's Germany and its criminals. An SS who went over to restrain her rage, was violently slapped in the face by her. It was the most beautiful thing I had ever seen in the camp.

Soon after, singing the "Hymn to Freedom," Malla raised her hands, red with blood, for she had succeeded in cutting the veins of her wrists. In spite of it, the hangmen pulled her, fallen and half-dead, under the gallows. Fortunately, however, she died before they had time to hang her. In the end they took her to the crematorium, to the furnace.

Then our own punishment followed. Everyone in the *Lager* went without water for three days, and in addition, on the following day, we had to remain standing for hours. I don't remember how many hours because they seemed endless. They forced us into a very tiring position: our eyes turned toward the bright sun; both hands raised holding two bricks; and even then, one foot of the two held up high — never ever both down. In this awkward position, threatened and beaten by the guards, all the prisoners were paying for Malla's illegal action and near escape.

Aussenkommando

Every morning on our way to work, we passed by male prisoners from a camp for men not far from ours. In any case, they were sharing the same fate we were, and often times we would do the same work. When they were nearby, only the barbed wire separated us, and at lunchtime we were permitted to talk freely with them.

During that time, I ran along the barbed wire asking if any Greeks were there. Then I was asking the Greeks whether there were any Kastorians among them. I was very anxious to learn about the 320 young men whom they had selected together with me at the station the day of our arrival in Auschwitz. Who they were and what happened to them? But no one knew anything. Apparently that whole group of young Kastorians had been moved to another camp.

Every moment I wondered and worried whether my younger

---

*Germaine reminded me of this shocking event (which, of course, I had never forgotten) as well as the name of Malla, which I did not recall.

A Cry for Tomorrow 76859 ...

brother Alberto was alive, and my uncle Zahos too. And my cousins who were still young boys and some of the others? Where had they been taken?

In my women's group there were two sisters from Thessaloniki — Lena and Aliki Kapon — two very nice girls with whom I used to talk all day. In our general misfortune, Lena and Aliki proved to be the most fortunate in the *Lager*. Their case was very rare. Every morning when we would go to work they became very emotional because at the place we worked they could see their father and brother in the men's group. This meant that of their immediate family of five — mother, father, two sisters, and a brother — only the mother who went directly to the crematorium was missing. The rest were alive in the camp, even doing the same work as we.

Every time I saw this scene I'd go to Papa Kapon whom I identified with my own father, as they were about the same age. Each time I would tell him he was just like mine. I remember giving him a little bread a couple of times from my own small portion.

These everyday scenes were so full of emotion. As soon as we arrived at work, our eyes would spontaneously look across to the opposite side of the barbed wire, as all the men fixed their eyes on us.

Little by little a familiarity developed, and we would look for each other. These faces, seen daily, even without being acquainted, soon became family. In the beginning a smile, then interest, then human concern, maybe love. Each of us women chose a male who would at least be over there, and could be seen again the next day, even from a distance. And that person would tell her perhaps to be patient, or that who knows, or that last night I was thinking of you because you gave me courage. And maybe he would even say to you, "Hold on for me, please don't die. I want to see you alive tomorrow and the day after tomorrow."

How sensitive human nature is! Even in this horrible state, deep inside our emaciated bodies were stirrings of some very strange feelings. Is it possible that life's instinct to survive springs from a spark of love to warm the lifeless body, revive it little by little, so it holds on to life and does not let it die?

All prisoners of the camp began using the same expression: "My *Cohan* over there," they would say, meaning "my beloved." Those who had been there longer would say, "I'm his *Cohana*," meaning "that prisoner loves me."

Once, a girl next to me asked who my *Cohan* was. I looked around to find one in the distance that very moment (that's how it would happen), as I didn't have anybody over there. Suddenly, my stomach churned and I felt all my beautiful girlish dreams dissolve in an instant — dreams I had so eagerly and joyfully waited to come true. For at that moment, as I looked to find somebody for me among the boys over there, I only saw men standing with shaven skulls and sunken eyes.

"I can't find anyone," I replied. "I don't know, can't choose, maybe some other time, not today anyway."

But most of the girls could.

That same evening, upon returning to the Quarantine Block (No. 27), a *Stubenoberst,* "assistant," was waiting for me, smiling. She was the assistant to the *Blockoberst* in the kitchen and responsible for evening food distribution. In the evening they handed out the bread with a little margarine and a spoonful of marmalade or a little bad smelling cheese. The portions intended for us, already small, became smaller as they passed from hand to hand. This was because every superior working in food delivery or distribution — *Kapo, Blockoberst, Stubenoberst* — was stealing, each in turn, and saving food for themselves and their gang or those who protected them. Their surplus was exchanged for cigarettes or whatever else they needed. So a black market trade ring evolved with its own secret network. It started inside the camp and spread outside to Polish citizens.

This *Stubenoberst* was a Polish Jew (I don't remember her name). She liked me a lot and said she wanted us to become friends. She asked me which language I knew that she spoke, so we could communicate. I told her I didn't know German yet or even Polish. I'm Greek, I said. Finally though, when I tried to say something in Hebrew from what I had learned in my primary Jewish school, it worked. She knew a little, and I also realized she was very religious.

We enjoyed talking to each other. Since she was the *Stubenoberst* and I was aware she controlled the food, I made every effort possible to show her that I was very learned in religion, because religion was so important to her. (To tell the sad truth, I felt no shame then or even now as I am recalling this scene.) What's more, I sang little festival songs to her that I learned as a child. I wondered how they came to mind in the state I was in. The results were excellent. As I sang at the top of my lungs to pretend the vocal prima donna, her joy was such that she immediately rushed to the kitchen and brought me two big slices of bread with margarine and marmalade. I couldn't believe my eyes! First I grabbed them like a hungry animal and only later

A Cry for Tomorrow 76859 ...

remembered to thank her. At last, after so long, I had something more to eat that day.

I stared at that bread, stared at it again. First I brought it to my nose to smell it and nourish my heart before I tasted it. Then, before putting it into my mouth I remembered Dora and rushed to offer her a little of the unexpected I had won that day. In the beginning Dora categorically refused to take it. She didn't want to deprive me of it and said I didn't have to share it with anybody. I was so impressed how even with the bread under her nose she could refrain from putting it in her mouth. God, with the hunger that tortured us, how could she continue to have so much strength. Finally, I remember, she took a bit after I insisted and I ate the rest little by little to enjoy the pleasure. Finishing it, I went back to the *Stubenoberst* to express my feelings of gratitude to her in person.

Suddenly we heard the whistle and understood we had to go out for *Appell*, and that something was happening again. My Polish girlfriend told me not to join the opposite line where the newcomers usually stand. "It doesn't matter," she said. "If you stay here with the older ones for roll call, the final number of prisoners will still be the same. You can stay." So I happily stayed close by her and soon three more girls were added to complete the group of five. Standing at attention by groups in two lines, one opposite the other, we waited as always to be counted.

Indeed, something different was going on that day. Germans officials arrived including SS officers, even women SS — in blue uniform with stripes on their shoulders and black boots high up to their knees. These women were rosy and fat from plenty of food. They all moved as one body toward the older prisoners where I was also standing.

With their typical seriousness, they began selecting some of us women to work at another *Kommando*. When the girls saw what was happening, they immediately became excited and started begging the Germans to write down the number of their arm. I didn't understand anything, but the Slovak women, knowing better than I, shouted the words, *"Bitte, ich auch."* "Please me too."

As I listened to them, I started imitating them quietly without shouting, and I repeated the phrase I heard without understanding its meaning. *"Bitte, ich auch."* That was it! That instant, a German SS woman saw me, grabbed my arm and said, *"Ja-wohl, und du."* "Yes, you too for sure."

AUSCHWITZ

To my surprise and to the surprise of all the others, the number on my arm was decisively written down on their list together with only a few others. The list was then given to the *Blockoberst,* who was informed of what she had to do next.

"What is done is done. It cannot now be undone," they said. "Moreover, you are dealing with superiors here."

After these procedures, they all left: officers, Germans, German SS women, dogs. The yoke had been loosened, but I remained dumfounded.

"I don't understand a thing. What is happening?" I asked my Polish friend.

She was very happy for me and tried to explain that fate was smiling on me today because I had stood in the line of the older prisoners. They enrolled me to work in a good *Kommando,* beginning the next day. If I had been on the other side, they would never have chosen me, because I was a newcomer, she said.

"Where will they take me? I don't want to be separated from my people." I didn't understand why I had shouted. I had shouted *"und ich"* as a joke.

Upset and frightened, I started crying. I was in a state of panic. After a while, still upset, I first gathered Dora and then all my cousins and friends who were also worried about me. We appealed to Daisy, the *Blockoberst,* to intervene if possible and put somebody else in my place — someone who would like to change her job.

Daisy replied: "Impossible, nothing can be done now. Here everything is very strict. I could even lose my position."

"But as for you," she said to me, "why are you crying? As things are, you should be pleased right now, because you're lucky to be going there. You will eat well and be warmly dressed. All the women here envy your new job. Don't forget, you're the only newcomer who has been chosen. My sister Anna also works in that *Kommando* and she is very pleased."

I only knew one thing: that I would be leaving to go to some unknown block to stay and work far from my friends and the girls I knew.

Finally, Dora took me aside and with all her wisdom and usual logic tried in her gentle way to bring me around. "Look Berry," she said to me, "in this place we find ourselves, we aren't free to do as we wish. Each of us must manage alone, because in reality, each of us is alone. From now on we are going to be separated again and again.

A Cry for Tomorrow 76859 ...

Today you, tomorrow me. I hope you will at least be better off than here."

I couldn't sleep all night. I was nervous because I didn't know where they would be taking me the very next day.

Kanadakommando

The following day with a heavy heart I was separated from my friends and cousins and let myself be guided by my "superiors." Leaving Quarantine Block No. 27, they told me that in the evenings after *Appell,* when we were usually free for one or two hours, I could go and see my friends. We wouldn't be far apart. This was somewhat comforting to me, as I knew during that time, everybody in the women's camp was circulating and could go from one block to the other.

So very early in the morning we arrived at Block 1. The girls working in the *Effekten* or *Rotes Kanadakommando** lived there, they told us. Going in, I was bewildered by the girls I saw. Everyone looked neat and comfortable and didn't seem to be deprived of food.

From somewhere I heard Greek and Spanish and spontaneously turned in that direction. "Girls, are you Greek?" I asked. "How are things here?"

"Yes, Greek women from Thessaloniki. All together there are almost forty of us. Are you Greek? Where from? When did you arrive?" One after the other they started asking nostalgically for news of Greece. Apparently they had been in Auschwitz for one full year already.

"Come, welcome to our group," they said to me. "We'll be going to work together, and there you'll eat well and will recover quickly." Indeed, after forty days spent in the quarantine block, I was suffering such privation and prostration that I couldn't even recognize myself.

Right away they took my rags off me and dressed me in a uniform of coarse canvas with blue and white vertical stripes, and a red kerchief for my head. Here in *Kanadakommando* all the girls had to be uniformly dressed in striped prisoner uniform and a red kerchief on their head. (That's why it's called *Rotes Kanada,* they told me.) I

---

*At the *Effekten* is the way Kanada was referred to. In German it is the place where goods and chattel are kept. In short, it was the place where the robbed property of the inmates and the murdered where held. Rotes Kanadakommando means "Red Canada Commando" and the name grew out of black humor, probably because Canada represented a wealthy country to the prisoners.

finally felt somewhat tidy, and what I now put on better protected my weak and suffering body.

Still, the bane of my existence were my shoes, for I couldn't take one more step. The Greek girls comforted me immediately and told me to be patient until they took us to work and that there I'd find the best ones to put on! The truth is that all of them without exception, as far as I could tell, were wearing nice boots suitable for heavy walking, and this impressed me!

After a while I took a look at the bunk bed where I was to sleep at night. It was something else! The same bunks, of course, the same style as in the other blocks, but what a difference! Linen sheets on the bottom, feather quilts on top, silk pajamas, finest quality nightgowns. I thought I was dreaming. Yet, even though my eyes saw inexplicable comforts, my ears continued to hear the same shouting or worse than the ones of Block 27 that I had left shortly before.

"Hurry up," the Greek girls told me, "because here we have the worst *Blockoberst*. She's a Czechoslovak Jewess named Terca, who is cruel. Watch out for her ... don't give her any excuse. God help you if you fall into her hands."

We went out for *Appell* in our striped uniform and red kerchief. After counting us many times over we passed through the huge gate of the camp, five-five to a line stepping to the music of the orchestra. Accompanied by guards with their vicious dogs as always, we turned down an asphalt road that ended after walking about five or six kilometers.

"Here we are," the guards said. "Dismiss and start working quickly."

When we stopped, God, what met my eyes! Piles! Piles of luggage, thousands of suitcases bulging with things ... shoes of all kinds, women's, men's ... piles of women's dresses, men's suits, children's clothes, baby clothes. Mountains of eyeglasses, small, large, sunglasses. Piles of blankets, furs, sheets, linens, silk embroideries, lace. Canned goods of every kind, bread, sweets, boxes, and medicines....

I lost my breath. I grew conscious that all these things represented us — the thousands and millions of Jews driven from our homes and forcibly led here to Auschwitz and to Birkenau. At the nearby crematoria opposite me, I could see the flames burning them, burning our people.... And here below were their belongings, their things that were soon to be so useful to the Germans. A fantastic

A Cry for Tomorrow 76859 ...

fortune! Here in front of my eyes! Proof of an unbelievable treasure!

It's what these Jews brought and lugged all the way here with them with their own hands. The few cherished things of the poor, and even the jewels, diamonds, money, and other valuables of the rich. And we, Jews ourselves, standing before this inconceivable and freakish spectacle as *Kanadakommando*. What irony!

They ordered us to separate kind by kind, to distinguish one from the other, and with our own hands to make parcels to be sent immediately to the German people in Berlin by special train. In other words, our work was to search those huge piles, that jumble, and choose the right clothes that would then be arranged into parcels.

As for the valuables, the gold, diamonds, or money we would find among "our" clothes — strict order: throw them into the large white box with the long narrow slot on top (so no hand could fit in). Only to be opened by officers authorized to take the contents with them.

I was dazed and could not recover from what I was seeing. I leaned my head against something and sought some reasonable meaning ... but couldn't find one. On the contrary, I went mad and felt like shouting, crying, killing, killing myself.

For a moment I saw myself as a wild beast again and it frightened me. I was sickened by rage and I don't remember how I finished my first day there. Apparently I remained in this state until that night when they pushed me like an automaton onto the bunk bed they had shown me. Insensibly I slipped underneath the warm and feathery blanket and fell asleep until dawn of the next day.

> "Man is an animal whom we can treat as we please, a being able to get used to anything."
>
> —*Dostoevsky*

Next morning after joining the line with my newly acquired Greek girls, I knew I had to find another formula at this new work in order to survive. Too much logic didn't work in the jungle of the camp. Neither did too much madness, like yesterday's crisis that could have easily killed me. I had no choice. Whether I wanted to or not, I would have to gradually adopt the psychology of the *Kanadakommando* girls who had been there a year or more already.

So that I would recover, these girls forced me to eat well from the food that was in abundance there, or that arrived the previous day with the train carrying Jews. They also told me to change my shoes as soon as possible to be able to walk. Little by little with compassion and kindness they helped me adjust to my new situation.

Every day as soon as we arrived at work, they told us to take off our striped uniform and red kerchief and hang them up somewhere. During work hours, we alone had the privilege of wearing whatever warm clothes we wanted — pants, sweaters, dresses, etc. Then in the afternoon they ordered us to put our uniform on again for the return to Block 1 where we slept.

So after work — washed up and clean for our return — we put on the striped uniform again before passing through "control." Control consisted of four to five superior *Kapos* who were supposedly trusted by the Germans. Three or four officers, positioned opposite us, observed these *Kapos* from a distance to be sure the search on us was thorough. They feared we might carry some of the desirable goods on us for the benefit of other prisoners in the camp who were starving and dressed in rags. The Germans themselves, however, never searched us.

In the afternoons of the first days, I ran to Block 27 after *Appell* to see my Kastorian friends and cousins, and every afternoon for a week, I exchanged my cousins' shoes. I took their old clogs, put them on, and left them my new ones. What I did was very dangerous, because every morning before leaving for work, they checked to see if we were wearing clogs, as they knew what the girls of *Kanada* were doing. Had they caught me, they would have sent me back to *Aussenkommando* or to some other hellish place!

Gradually I caught on and grasped what was happening at our work just before control.

One day, a *Kapo* who had her eyes on me all morning, approached me, saying: "Hey you, little Greek girl, would you like to get these pajamas out through control for me this afternoon?" They were a pair of green and white striped pajamas, I remember.

"Look here," she said. "On your way out this afternoon, queue in my line and pass before me for "control." Put them in your panties or in your girdle." (We *Kanada* girls were allowed to wear girdles.) "Put on something for yourself as well, whatever you like, and when I search you, I'll pretend to find nothing."

I took it for her, of course, feeling terror and fright though as I passed through. *Kapos*, afraid of losing their positions didn't take risks themselves, so they got us to take out their things. Almost all of them turned a blind eye when frisking us. Many times their hands touched what we had hidden, but fortunately no one betrayed us.

A Cry for Tomorrow 76859 ...

This explains everything that was in Block 1: our linen sheets, pajamas, nightgowns, even feather quilts. The Slovak girls had another special way. They took things out by placing them in a small bundle near the door. Passing through control, they went through the door and grabbed the bundle when nobody was looking. Then they hid the bundle by passing it from one to the other in their row of five as they marched into the camp.

Almost the whole camp gathered outside Block 1 at night. *Blockobersten, Kapos* from all *Kommandos,* and *Stubenobersten* came to buy what we had stolen and brought from *Kanada.* An unprecedented trade took place there: with cigarettes, with gold, with food, with money. In the *Lager,* if bread was common currency, cigarettes were equivalent to gold.

These things were destined for the big heads of the camp, for the German, Czech, Polish, and Slovak women. Many were in on the game. A certain Frau Schmidt, a prisoner who herself had many privileges, seeing these vile women promenading around the court of wonders (*Kanada*) chased them, beat them, at which they ran away.

I limited myself to bringing a few things out from time to time. I was not interested in the trade nor ever learned how it operated. What I was interested in was helping the girls of "27" whenever I could. I remember one day I took a whole loaf of bread to them. Other times a little soap so they could wash somehow. Another time they asked me for some sugar for one of our own Kastorian girls sick with a high fever and I brought her sugar and aspirins. I brought them many other things, as well, whatever they asked me for.

Because the women of the other blocks were jealous, poor things, and had every right to be, they spoke of the *Kanada* girls as being gaudy, repulsive and heavy smokers, though they were well-groomed, well dressed, made-up, clean, and full of laughter. Unfortunately, however, reality had not changed. The danger of the crematorium was ever present for all without exception.

They exterminated the Gypsies

On another day, Germaine Cohen and all the others speaking as one voice, related to me how they did not go to *Aussenkommando* for work that day, but to the Gypsy barracks to clean them. The Gypsies, they said, lived as a group with their families and children somewhere nearby.

When they went in, Germaine said, "the barracks were empty,

but full of adult and children's clothing. There was a disarray of human activity: scattered plates with uneaten food, half-opened tins of milk, spilled fresh food, woolens, sweaters, underwear ... blood ... vomit ... even children's toys! Coerced and threatened, we cleaned, but asked ourselves: "What could have happened to all these people who had been here shortly before? They just disappeared?"

I quote from the book *Playing for Time** by Fania Fénelon, of an event that coincidentally we experienced at exactly the same period at Auschwitz-Birkenau:

> Hardly had we come back than we heard trucks driving through the rain. No train had arrived, so we had no idea who they were looking for. In the morning we learned that it had been the Gypsies from Hungary. They had been camping some distance away, on the other side of the men's camp. One morning, surrounded by SS, they had arrived with their wagons, their luggage, their old people, their women, children, and animals. They had set up their caravans, organized their camps, and they'd been living there for months, years perhaps. It was said that through the agency of a neutral country, the Americans had come to an agreement about the Gypsies, that they were paying for them to be kept alive. They used to sing and play the guitar; some evenings the air carried the sounds right to us, or so we thought. It was said that the SS killed them because their "allowance" hadn't arrived on time. The only certain thing was that they were gassed on the night of the black triangles' party. Probably the SS said nothing about it and continued to receive money for them until the camp was liberated.

Working in *Kanada*

The trains arrived one after the other every day from all over Europe. So naturally, the work in *Kanada* increased. We could hardly keep up with sorting and arranging the incredible amount of articles scattered and heaped on the ground.

At that time, five hundred girls were working during the day and three hundred at night. Every fifteen days the shift changed: the night shift worked during the day and the day shift worked at night. Men were also working with us.

The girls spontaneously separated into ethnic groups as they had

---

*Playing for Time by Fania Fénelon with Marcelle Routier, translated from the French by Judith Landry. Atheneum, New York, 1977, pp. 221-222.

things in common, especially their language. The French girls liked the creams, the aromas, the make-up, and were always perfumed, ready for flirting. On the other hand, the Polish girls, not known for their cleanliness, were called *"brudny,"* which means "dirty" in Polish, but I don't know why. The Czechoslovack women were dynamic and we were a little afraid of them because almost all were *Kapos*. As for us Greek girls, everybody in the *Lager* called us *Greco, klepsi-klepsi* using the Greek word for "stealing"!

Naturally, I worked side by side with the Greek girls who had befriended me from the first moment: Frieda Medina, who had the mind of a mature and logical woman; Suzy, a lovely girl with clever blue eyes; and Erica. Erica had close ties with Alegra Kamhi. Alegra was the one who kept our morale high and was the wisest of all. Then there was Mary, who blushed every time she spoke, but was good-hearted and brave, and Nina Avayou, whom I admired very much.

Included also were the two sisters, Lisa and Marie. Marie was a very beautiful girl. As I marched with her in the line, she told me everything about her life. She said she was married but didn't know where her husband was. They had arrived here together and she wondered whether he was still alive.

The youngest of us all was Olga — that's what they called her at home — a brunette with blue eyes who danced very beautifully. Finally, there was Sarika la Evréa. She talked constantly about food and recipes. Every day in her imagination she was cooking us a different "speciality."

All these girls* were Thessalonikians. As for Greek men, we had René Molho and Sam Ezrati, both from Thessaloniki, and a certain Benico from eastern Thrace.**

At work, they separated us into two groups: the *Staplerinnen*, or "table-girls," who each folded and made up forty packets a day working at long narrow tables; and the *Lumpensammlerinnen* (from

---

*Almost all the Greek women who worked in *Kanada* survived: Frieda Medina, Suzy, Olga, and Sarika live in Israel. Of them, I meet Olga often. She is married with children. Alegra Kamhi? Hers is a most moving story, which is told here in the section "Life and death scenarios." Nina Avayou is married with children and lives in Athens. We see each other frequently, for she is the Secretary of the Union of Prisoners, of which I am currently the President. Erica is married and living in Thessaloniki. We communicate very often. She has two children and grandchildren.

**Of the three men, two survived: Rene Molho, who lives in Oakland, California, and Sam Ezrati, a successful family man who lives in New York.

"ragpicker" in German), who searched and chose the goods and clothes from the piles for the packets.

Each table-girl had two or three *Lumpensammlerinnen* as her assistants. From the beginning, I preferred to be a *Lumpensammlerin* to avoid making up the packets. One day as I moved among the piles searching for things. I found a bedspread embroidered in cross-stitch of various colored threads: beige, beautiful rose red, as well as pink. It was part of my cousin Rebecca Zacharia's dowry! How many summers in Kastoria had we spent embroidering this cover? How many times had I helped her, sitting next to her? We chatted about it, embroidered it, admired it.

In our eyes it was a "masterpiece," something so unusual! Who would ever imagine it would end up here, thrown in the piles at Auschwitz! Since that time, I could never again use cross-stitch for embroideries. And it was the only thing I recognized that had been dragged from Kastoria to which I felt I belonged.

"*Schnell! Schnell arbeiten!*" "Quickly! Work quickly!" the *Kapos* were shouting in my ears.

Truly, I shouldn't lose time. The *Staplerinnen* are dependent on me to bring them clothes for the packets. I mustn't delay or become distracted by my emotions.

During noon lunch the Greek group — men and women — ate together from the canned food we collected in the piles. Whatever we found collectively we gave to Sarika la Evréa to prepare the menu for us. "Today I have canned meat," she would tell us, or "today I have canned sardines," etc. And since at noon we were no longer drinking the *Lager* soup with its medicine, little by little our periods came back and at least we felt biologically all right.

Stressful moments

One afternoon after *Appell*, they took us from Block 1 directly to the decontamination building. There we had to hand over our striped uniform and our underwear all tied with a belt, to be disinfected in the kilns. Then we entered a large hall - five hundred women — and waited completely naked as when our mothers gave birth to us, until we got our disinfected clothes back.

It was a very brutish experience! We talked ... we spoke ... we remained silent, we grew anxious. Time seemed to stand still. Unable to endure the fatigue, our weak naked bodies began falling down on the cement floor. This lasted more than twelve hours until morning, when we heard them calling the numbers on our arms for they had also been sewn on our clothes.

The clothes we received back (I can see them at this very moment) were still soaking wet and steaming from the kiln. When we tried to dress, they stuck to our bodies and wouldn't go on. Like this, sleepless and in wet clothes, they took us directly to work. Without having slept at all, my exhaustion at the time is impossible to describe. At work I dragged myself around in a drowsy state, hearing the voices of the *Kapos* shout, *"Schnell, Schnell arbeiten!"*

I was supposed to search in the piles of clothes and take what I chose to the table-girls waiting to make the packets. For a moment I didn't know where I was going. I couldn't see anymore and it became impossible to keep my eyes open. Without realizing it I fell down like a corpse, slipped inside the warm piles of clothes and surrendered to deserved sleep. I slept deeply, very deeply, and apparently was snoring from weariness.

The girl who stood at the door of the barrack (*Kapos* placed a girl there as a guard) started shouting: *"vingt-deux ... vingt-deux,"* meaning "twenty-two" in French. This word was the signal that some superior officer was approaching for control. It happened two or three times a day. The *"vingt-deux"* was transmitted like wireless from mouth to mouth and all the girls would run obediently to occupy their fixed work positions.

All talking stopped.... A great silence reigned as was usual in these circumstances.

And then, lo and behold, *Unterscharführer* Gruber came in — a tall, blue-eyed, blonde man whose boots shook the universe as he walked.

At precisely that moment, something unheard of happened! In the barrack, in that great stillness and silence during the time Gruber was present for the control, my loud snoring was heard — a rattle so penetrating and unusual that it worried Gruber himself.

"What is going on in this barrack?" he shouted. "Something's going on here ... but what?"

The girls and the *Kapos* were crazed with fear and nobody moved from their place. Gruber, glancing round and round, resolutely approached the place where I was, where the snoring was coming from. Just before reaching me, a Greek girl, realizing that I was sleeping somewhere there, immediately jumped like a whirlwind onto the clothes, stuck her hand inside, grabbed my hair, pulled it hard, and whispered to me in Greek, "Wake up quickly but don't move. Stay there, as you are, and don't come out until I tell you to."

My head ached as she kept pulling my hair very hard to immobilize me....

"Yes," grandfather said to me, who I was still dreaming about at that moment. "Don't be afraid, my child, be patient. It will soon be over. Stay quiet as they tell you to."

Even now when I recall this event and the dream with my grandfather, I still shake.

Gruber didn't understand how the inexplicable noise, which lasted so long, had stopped so suddenly. He went out hastily to call for military assistance. Meanwhile, my Greek friend helped me get up, told me to quickly go inside and wash where there was a little water, gave me a comb to fix my hair, and told me to tidy up. Then I was to hurry to my work place as if I'd been busy there for some time.

My heart was beating wildly as I tried to do it all in time. When Gruber came back in with three or four armed SS I was all right, only swollen from sleep.

They lined us up, conducted roll call, counting us over and over. They verified for themselves that nobody was missing. Moreover, no sounds were heard any more. So they all left, though still a little suspicious.

At last I breathed. God, what a day again!

Control upon control

The Germans of our camp grew very irritated because the arrivals of Jews started decreasing. In retaliation, they played a nasty game on us *Kanada* girls.

One afternoon after work, having passed through our usual control, having gone out in rows of five, and even having started our march down the asphalt road for Birkenau, we suddenly saw military maneuvers in the distance.

"What the devil is happening?" we murmured to each other, frightened.

Motorcycles, cars, officers, women SS! They stopped us abruptly, ordering us to pass in front of them one by one almost naked, with the striped uniform in our hands. It was a second control! *"Schnell! Schnell!"* they shouted.

The five hundred women, separated into five groups of one

hundred, were now in the very middle of the road. We Greek girls found ourselves about the second to the last group of one hundred.

We soon learned it was a surprise control set up by the Germans. Worried *Kapos* paced to-and-fro. The women in the first rows who could, escaped and ran to warn the last ones of the oncoming danger. "Hurry up," they said. "Drop whatever you have on you or they'll catch you too."

Being among the last, we believed if we hurried we'd have just enough time to throw everything away. So with hearts in our throats, that's what we did. We dropped everything off of us. Then, striped uniform in hand, we ran obediently and passed one by one in front of the Germans as if nothing had happened.

After one or two hours of this procedure, having finally passed this additional control, I turned around for a moment to look at the road we were leaving behind with my own eyes. Five hundred women loaded with clothes, breads, colognes, blankets, pajamas, nightgowns, canned food, cigarettes, dollars, diamonds, tins of oil, and whatever else the human mind can imagine, had thrown everything down on the asphalt road. The road from one end to the other — its entire length — had filled with goods in a flash. And these were the goods brought into the camp every afternoon by us, the girls of *Kanada*.

Extremely angry, the Germans punished 200 women caught red-handed with stolen items. They immediately removed them from *Kanada* and sent them to *Aussenkommando* or other worse places. Apparently their plan was to decrease the number of workers in *Kanada* that very day.

We Greek girls stayed with the remaining 300 on the day shift and went on working in *Kanada,* very shaken by what had happened, waiting for our turn to come someday.

Soulless diamonds

Even our days in *Kanada* passed with anguish, stress, and anxiety.

My *Staplerin* asked me to search and find her ten dresses of the same quality, wool or silk if possible. Each packet was to contain ten pieces of the same kind, so she shouted again: "I want ten sweaters now, and all must be woolen or silk!"

"How can I find the items you ask for? Where do you think we are? Have you forgotten? And if you mix them up a bit, why do you care? Damn them!" I shouted, "They want everything perfect! Enough is enough."

"You know I can't mix things up because every packet is checked," she said to me. "Don't you know we take them first to a table where four or five *Kapos* are responsible? They check the contents, approve them, note the number of our arm, and verify I brought her 1, 2, 3, 4, 5, 10 up to the forty packets required of each of us. After the control check we throw them in that corner over there which you see like a storage area, and from there they send them directly to Berlin."

My mind didn't care for the explanations.... As for me, I wasn't very productive at my work, because I was curious about everything that fell into my hand. For each thing I invented a different story: "How beautiful this dress is!" I would say. "The poor woman who wore it must have been slim and blond. Look, even a strand of blond hair on it. I was right! The hemline seems heavy ... let me undo it a little, now that nobody's looking." Very cautiously, I might remove a gold chain....

"This other dress is heavy. Let's see what's in the padding and inside this bulge tied with buttons...." Out of the padding might come lots of folded paper money — bank notes from the owner's country of origin. And inside the tied buttons ... oftentimes white diamonds, green emeralds, blue and white sapphires, red rubies!

This made my blood boil. Carefully, so nobody would notice, I would separate myself little by little, go outside supposedly to pee, holding the valuables tightly in my hand. Then with a spoon for a shovel, I would dig in the ground and put them in holes to completely hide them. I never threw anything into the white box we had in the middle of the barracks for the Germans.

Each time I was disturbed by similar feelings, but after much thought I came to the conclusion that these things which once represented a fabulous fortune, now at least, have no value for us anymore. All this gold, the diamonds that fall into our hands have no meaning or purpose in this hell where we find ourselves. They are completely soulless ... useless.

In my vexed imagination, I sometimes saw myself hopeless to the point of being dead. That I was somewhere up high in heaven looking down on earth observing grown-up people playing games with these stones called diamonds, asking myself: For these they quarrel and kill each other? For these they make wars? For these so much hatred and so many catastrophes?

A Cry for Tomorrow 76859 ...

The dangerous trick

The German governors of Auschwitz and Birkenau were becoming very nervous. They were coming and going and appeared more and more at our work. By all means something serious was happening about which we didn't yet know, but expected to learn from moment to moment, as all news circulated very quickly in the camp from mouth to mouth, from block to block, from the oldest to the youngest.

Finally one day at work, a superior officer, the *Obersturmführer*, arrived to inspect our camp. Most probably this was Joseph Kramer, a tall, fat, horrible man, as I remember. He sat outside in the open at the middle of a table surrounded by five or six other officers all talking seriously together. They took us out of the work blocks and lined us up at attention in rows of five. We listened to their orders.

"Today we decided to transfer some of you out to *Aussenkommando*. For the time being, all *Kapos* and *Staplerinnen* will stay here in *Kanada*. The rest of you and other assistants will leave immediately for other *Kommandos*. Be careful, we don't want arguments and commotion, or you will pay for it."

I was deathly afraid. Though I wasn't a trapeze artist, I could easily adapt in a hurry to other conditions. I was extremely worried.

At that they began counting the *Staplerinnen* and the number they wanted to retain was almost the same. Suddenly, officers began shouting in the distance wanting two more to fill in. You had to hurry to their table and register your number. At that moment, my Greek *Staplerin* pushed me to run and get signed up before others.

Oh God, what a melee! As soon as they understood, the other girls like me fell one on top of the other like wild animals, trying to get there first. Soon we were all tangled together, fighting one another. Moreover, this was the game of the Germans. They deliberately provoked such situations and were delighted to see us fighting among ourselves.

Then the guards loosed the dogs and any of us could have met our end. But this time, I alone had a brush with death. Without realizing how, I was down with a dog on top of me.

Meanwhile, whistles and clubs dispersed the crowd. All who could flee fled, running anywhere to save themselves. But I, I was on the ground, unable to move at all.

Seeing me down, the *Obersturmführer* finally decided to order the other officers to stand me up and take me to his table. He asked me for the number on my arm and told me in German that it's okay, I would remain at work in *Kanada*.

Was this also part of their game, or did he feel sorry for me? In any case, the following day I became a *Kanadakommando Staplerin* making forty packets a day at those long narrow tables.

Little by little we suspected the truth when the piles of clothes began decreasing and there were not as many things as in the first months. The transports of Jews became fewer and fewer. And as the loads did not arrive, our German supervisors became all the more stubborn and unyielding. Whether or not there were goods, they said, we still had to supply forty packets a day each.

We were in a difficult position and our packets became our daily nightmare ... until one day, we Greek girls improvised a trick, as there was no alternative — the *klepsi-klepsi* trick. Besides, we had the name anyway. "*Greco, klepsi-klepsi,*" they called us.

I recall we put this dangerous trick into practice and just took our chances. It worked like this: When the packet was ready we took it for checking. After it was checked, a friend of ours kept watch. If no one was looking, this friend would say in Greek: "Okay, come now, bring the packet back to your table." If a *Kapo* was watching she said, "Watch out!" in which case the packet went to the storage room.

In this way, we took the same packets for checking again and again, until forty packets were counted. This trick worked fine for several days. Eventually almost all the *Staplerinnen* copied us and did the same.

Soon though, when the Germans came to take the packets from storage for shipping them to Berlin, they looked puzzled over the fact that the packets were not as many as those registered on *Kapo* lists. Furious, they immediately ordered a control to recount the packets in front of them. I remember two Germans, one opposite the other, counting the packets one by one and throwing them from one side to the other: *Eins-zwei-drei....*

All the girls gathered around them to follow the counting. One *Kapo*, who was chiefly responsible and more in danger than anybody else, motioned to us and secretively proposed that we steal the packets which had already been counted and bring them in again from the other side to be recounted.

Behind their backs, three or four girls ran like mice and we carefully covered for them. They managed to bring packets back that were already counted. The Germans focused only in front of them, lest they miss any during their counting. We watched and suffered from anxiety, but in the end it finally came out correct.

A Cry for Tomorrow 76859 ...

Life and death scenarios

Every day things became more difficult. We believed that an end was approaching, but at the same time we were afraid our end was approaching also.

"What do you think," I asked my friend Alegra Kamhi one day. "Do you think we'll get out of here alive, or we'll die too as so many millions who pass through the chimneys?"

"No, Berry dear, we won't die," she replied.

Alegra always had a smile on her face and a kind word on her lips — besides, Alegra in Spanish means "joy".

"Look," she continued, "I will tell you something to convince you that you will get out of here. Take me for instance. I had many brothers and sisters and most of them died in car accidents or something similar, one after the other. You see there's a curse on our family which means we will all leave this world in the same manner! And I, you see, believe I'll die like that one day too. I'm telling you, I believe it without a doubt. It's not this crematorium that will kill me. You'll see! I'll get out of here for sure and be killed somewhere outside the camp. There are no cars here, so how can I be killed? Berry dear, since I'll get out of here, you'll surely get out of here too. I want you to believe that."

At the moment Alegra and I were discussing these things, her close friend Erica arrived. Listening to us she started laughing. "Didn't I tell you, Berry dear, that my love, Rufus, is waiting for me in Thessaloniki?" Erica said. "You'll see, Rufus and I will meet for sure one day again. He told me he'll be waiting for me and I believe that's how it's going to happen!"

This was the daily conversation of these two girls. We lived together and day and night I heard that Rufus was waiting for Erica and that Alegra would die in an accident.

Both were saved from the crematorium.

As soon as Erica was liberated, she went to Thessaloniki where she met her Rufus and married him. One day after the war as soon as I met Erica again, I asked her: "Well, what about Rufus?"

"Come," she said, "let me introduce you to him. Didn't I tell you so?"

As for Alegra, on her way back after her liberation, she met a young Jew named Alfredo Melamet somewhere in Noestad. They fell in love and decided to eventually marry. One day Alfredo said to her: "Get up on the back of my motorcycle, we'll go for a nice ride." Alegra happily agreed. As she was holding on behind Alfredo, she lost her balance, fell from the motorcycle, and was dragged under its wheels for a time until she died. Alegra left this world forever in the way she firmly believed she would.

The "premium"

Unterscharführer Gruber was the officer in charge, and each day he came for the control. Every time I saw him I shivered with fear, thinking of the day I was snoring under the piles of clothes and of the danger I had put myself in.

When he saw me, he seemed to remember the other event that took place in his presence. The time I was overcome by the guard and dog and then kept in *Kanada*. Every time he passed by me, he smiled at me as if telling me, "Yes, I know you now." But my heart knew how much better it would be if he didn't know me at all!

One day, as soon as he came into the block where we were working, he went directly to the *Kapo* and gave her a packet of coupons. "Premiums." The Germans used to give them to prisoners who stood out for good work. Each coupon was valid for buying small extras from the *Lager* canteen such as a cucumber, a pickle, a carrot or a little marmalade, etc. To be entitled to a premium one had to work very hard for weeks. We who worked in *Kanada* were not impressed by the premium, because at our work, we had many more goods than the few things offered by the canteen.

Well, that day Gruber ordered the *Kapo* to distribute them to the best *Staplerinnen*. As soon as he gave her the packet, he sat on a chair near the *Kapo's* table to personally observe the girls receiving the premiums. Gruber for the first time sat there for hours and waited. I noticed that from time to time he turned his head toward me, watching my movements.

Innocent me, I didn't move from my place. I worked silently and wasn't interested in the premium. After the *Kapo* distributed some, she said she had two or three left and announced whoever wanted one to come and take it.

I was still at my place making packets ... when I suddenly felt Gruber's eyes persistently fixed on me, as if immobilizing me. A strong feeling came over me and suddenly the thought passed through my mind that something serious was happening again.

Instinctively I jumped, ran quickly toward the *Kapo* like a whirlwind, telling her I wanted a premium. And soon as I took it in my hand and the *Kapo* wrote my number down, Gruber seemed satisfied, smiled at me again, rose suddenly and left the room without saying a word to me.

A few minutes later, the *Kapo* and the German officers were heard shouting at us to get in line and listen to the latest announcement. "Official Order: All *Staplerinnen* who got a premium remain in *Kanadakommando*. The rest, without any discussion, leave for other *Kommandos* elsewhere.

I was speechless! I myself couldn't believe what was happening. And now all my Greek girlfriends left, and despite the fact that I was staying in the *Kommando* with eighty other girls, I felt alone again without the Greek girls I was accustomed to. And who could believe that only a few months ago, eight hundred of us were working there day and night?

Brezinka

That same night we abandoned Block 1 of Birkenau and the last eighty women were led to Brezinka, an annex of Auschwitz next to Crematorium IV. From that day, I couldn't see my Kastorian girl friends of Block 27 whom I used to see almost every afternoon. I was also separated from my friends Lena, Rita, and Dora, as well as from my cousins, Gita and Regina.

Moreover, I entered a new camp where I was confined without freedom of movement anymore. On the other hand, they completely took away our striped uniform and we put on whatever clothes we found at work.

On the road just before entering Brezinka, I was almost paralyzed by shock again. That which met our eyes was something indescribably horrifying. Along the way, on the left and on the right, we saw piles of human skeletons like matchsticks in rows heaped one on top of the other. They were frozen bodies preserved by the cold and the snow that continuously fell on them. A little farther on were the crematoria that apparently were not able to handle all the burning — either because the corpses were too many, or because some machine of the crematorium had broken down. Until it was fixed, 10,000 to 20,000 corpses were waiting their turn to go into the furnace.

In this manner we entered Brezinka, five-five in line surrounded by this horror of death. When we stopped at our barrack and glanced around us, we realized that there were four crematoria in the area. But the one we would see day and night was the one exactly opposite us — Crematorium IV.

Across from the crematorium was an open courtyard where every

AUSCHWITZ

morning we women would shower completely naked in freezing cold water. The first days I shivered terribly from the freezing water falling on my body. But little by little, watching the Czechoslovak girls endure it, we ever so slowly imitated them and somewhat adjusted to the cold! Moreover, after the freezing shower we felt better.

While we were washing, German officers came into the courtyard every day to entertain themselves. They enjoyed our shivering and most of all our nakedness. They viewed us as unsightly animals, though they didn't touch us — just tried to humiliate and ridicule our femininity. Nothing else.

In the beginning, this morning scene with them bothered me, and every time I saw them, I tried to cover my nudity. But then I suddenly decided to act as if they weren't there. I told myself these people are neither human nor animals.

Our work here at first was the same as in *Kanada* and we made the same forty packets a day. Then it changed and became somewhat different. We didn't make packets anymore, but filled bundles with rags cut into strips from useless dresses or other clothes which could not be worn. I don't remember how many bundles each of us had to fill in a day.

The barracks were full of bundles destined for another *Kommando* called "Viberay." There, other women were braiding those rags into stuffings used in airplanes. At least that's what was rumored.

A voice from *Sonderkommando*

Every day something shattering, every day a new shock to remind us that we were living in hell. One day, a Greek who worked inside the crematorium opposite, sang loudly in Greek and we could hear him. This voice will stay deep in my soul as long as I live. It was an anonymous male voice singing and crying out every night from Crematorium IV, reciting his suffering in these words:

> Greek girls
> who hear me
> tra-la-la-la-la
>
> I'm singing this as song
> so you won't get me wrong.
>
> The chimneys up far,
> do you know what they are?

111

A Cry for Tomorrow 76859 ...

They're factories of Death.
That's what they are.

Thousands of Jews
all without blame
old, young, and children
in the arms of the flame

Soon non-existent
burnt I will be,
unable to tell
what my tired eyes see.

Girls, can you hear me?
the horror is true
please now believe me
I live it as a Jew.

Greek girls, please
if one day you get out,
explain to the world
what I'm singing about.

I learned this song by heart. I bring his words to these pages of mine to be read by my readers, just as he urged me to do:

explain to the world
what I'm singing about.

Forty braidings a day

After fifteen or twenty days in the general grimness of that environment, I had a pleasant surprise. My Greek girlfriends who had been taken in the last batch from *Kanada,* all came back to Brezinka! My joy was great as I was feeling so lonely, and now I would be working again side by side with Erica, Alegra, Sarika la Evréa, Mati, and all the others. They told me they had been working in Viberay ever since they left *Kanada.*

Erica had been shaken by a terrible incident that befell her at work there, and couldn't get over it for days. She told me that in Viberay she braided stuffings and had to turn in forty braidings a day. Well, one day shortly before her shift finished, the Kapo, a Jewish man from Thessaloniki, approached her and took the last braiding from her hand and undid it.

AUSCHWITZ

"No," Erica said to him, "please don't do this to me, I won't have time to braid it again, and if I don't turn in all forty braidings, they're going to punish me."

"I'm very sorry," he said, "you know I have to check all the windings to see if they're okay, that's why I'm a *Kapo*. This last braiding of yours isn't okay. You must do it over again."

He grabbed the braiding from her hand and deliberately undid it. Precisely at that moment the work shift ended and unfortunately, the Germans, realizing she had not turned in forty braidings, punished her severely by locking her in a bunker for almost four days without food and water.

She was almost forgotten in there. After three days and three nights, the *Kapo*, apparently feeling guilty, decided to remind the Germans to let her out. When she finally emerged half-dead, the *Kapo* had the nerve to tell her that it was really he who saved her, because he got her out of the bunker alive.

My hands

I was in the same barrack with Mati, a sweet, lovely girl with two small dimples on her cheeks, and we always got on well together. [She survived and I saw her recently.] While I liked her very much, I found her excessively clean — I'd say obsessively so — because she always had a small broom in her hand sweeping and sweeping the square space we were working in. Sometimes ten times an hour. I laughed at her constantly, telling her: "My dear, don't you realize where we are? Is cleanliness our only concern here?"

"Please don't talk to me like that," she replied. "Even here I want to feel that it's clean, at least in this space where I live."

There, where we were talking one day, lo and behold the *Kapo* appeared — a Polish shrew of a woman named Serenka. She disliked me very much and was always angry with me, for every time she saw me, she looked me over from top to bottom. This awful woman constantly called me "gorilla." Apparently, being very short, she was jealous of my height, for I was rather tall. She'd say to me, "Gorilla, you better work hard, or else."

So in addition to all the morbid and dangerous conditions surrounding us everywhere, Serenka had become a daily problem for me. I started worrying and didn't know how to deal with her. The only thing I managed to do was try to keep away from her, so at least she wouldn't see me.

One day as I was hiding behind the bundles avoiding her, pretending I was very occupied with work, I heard Serenka's voice asking Mati: "Where is the Gorilla? Go find her quickly and bring her here to me. I want her urgently."

Mati came looking for me, and as soon as she saw me, said: "Come quickly, Serenka is looking for you, and wants you to go to her immediately."

As soon as I appeared in front of her, her whole face lit up with joy. At her side stood Gruber, who, they said, came with an order, apparently from Dr. Mengele, to find the most beautiful hands among the girls who worked there. The girl who had the hands they were seeking would be taken by him to Block 10, the block for experiments.

Gruber realized that Serenka proposed me and was insisting that I was the one with the most beautiful hands of all. I noticed he let her have her way. He observed Serenka, being the *Kapo*, measuring my hands with a ruler from the one side ... from the other ... my fingers, my wrist..... Concluding, she exclaimed: "Exactly what they want!"

Finally, Gruber made up his mind, saying: "All right, I'll come another day for her hands." And he left, running out.

I stood there stunned and asked Serenka: "What is going on with my hands?"

"Haven't you understood yet, Gorilla?" she replied. "They're going to immortalize your hands, meaning, your hands are going to be mummified."

I didn't ask anything further. I thought a moment without saying anything to anybody. Are they only going to cut off my hands, or are they going to kill me to take my hands?

Gruber didn't appear again for a long time, and so this incident was forgotten for good. But I, I was in agony and anguished every second of every day that went by. Even now, when people say to me, "Berry, you have very beautiful hands," I cannot help but remember that horrible incident.

The alarm clock of the German guard

In the midst of all the commotion in the Brezinka camp, a pretty girl from Thessaloniki, Sarika Assael,* was going in and out of our barracks almost every day to visit the Greek girls.

---

*Sarika Assael (now Nahmia) lives in Thessaloniki today. She was a prisoner in the Auschwitz-Birkenau camp and her arm number was 42893

"How are things girls, how are you doing?" she would ask us.

"We are still alive," we replied. "And you, where are you working? Where do you stay?"

To that question of ours, Sarika always answered somewhat vaguely.

"Nearby, you see, a bit further down."

"Where do you mean, nearby?"

Sarika remained a question mark for me until I got the answer and that only recently. A short time ago, I purposely went to Thessaloniki to meet Erica, my friend and companion of our internment days. She helped me immeasurably to remember details from *Kanada* where we had worked together. Erica also invited Mati and Sarika to our meeting.

After talking for a while with the two other friends, it came time to speak with Sarika. I said to her: "I remember when you came to see us now and then, but I know very well that you were not one of the *Kanada* girls. So tell me now, where did you work at the time?"

Sarika answered me in a calm and very natural way, smiling sweetly as always. "I remember you very well, Berry. I saw you almost every day. Well, I was a kind of *Laufer* there, that is a "runner," going everywhere for whatever the *Kapos*, *Stubenobersten*, even the Germans wanted. There were eight girls doing this work. Apart from me, a Greek, the other seven were Slovaks. Sometimes we worked in the baths and received the newcomers. After having had their hair cut, we tattooed their arms. It was we who gave them the camp uniform and took away their good clothes, often finding fabulous fortunes in them.

Another time, you know, I had to perform a different job which was very difficult for me. I was the alarm clock of the German guard."

"What do you mean, 'alarm clock of the guard?'"

"You see," Sarika continued, "I had to wake up the German guard at a certain hour, that is, when the transports of Jews arrived at night from Europe. After the *Selektion* at the station, all those destined to be gassed had to be brought to the crematorium as quickly as possible. My orders were to go and wake up the guard, telling him: 'Wake up, the transport has arrived. Go and throw Zyklon B through the small window.' Zyklon B being the powder that would kill and asphyxiate so many people every day. You see, everything there was perfectly scheduled by the clock, to the minute, and everybody followed an order!"

I was stunned, and as I listened to her tell me all this, I confess I pitied her more than any other prisoner among us.

Sarika, now very upset, swore by her children (she has a daughter and grandchildren) as she continued to tell me the following:

"I want you to believe me, Berry dear, that every time I went to wake up the German guard, his belt with his revolver was thrown over a chair next to him. How many times my hand almost grabbed the revolver to kill him, instead of waking him up. But in the end I was never able to do it. And I've lived this nightmare a thousand times over. On the other hand, I secretly gave all the money and valuables that fell into my hands to the weakest prisoners to keep them alive, even in that hell of the camp. Maybe, I said to myself, one day they'll get out of here alive."

Warning from *Sonderkommando*

In the camp there was an international antifascist organization called, "The Resistance." This organization succeeded in collecting secret documents relating to the crimes of the SS. With the money and gold that circulated through *Kanada* and the crematoria, it was able to send messages to the outside world through Polish neighbors who were going in and out of the camp for work. Moreover, this organization saved prisoners' lives when it could and also helped prisoners bribe their way into a *Kommando* where the conditions were better.

These same people organized self-defense groups, even a conspiracy of the *Sonderkommando,* that is to say, among the men who worked inside the crematoria. It was the first days of October 1944, I recall....

One morning, there in the Brezinka camp where I was working, Sarika la Evréa came by and with surreptitious gestures, gathered all of us Greek girls of the *Kommando* together, saying she wanted to tell us something very serious and very secret.

We waited for the lunch hour so our meeting would seem more natural. Then, as we were sitting on the ground eating, Sarika la Evréa took a piece of paper from her breast and said in a low voice:

"Girls, listen carefully to what I'm going to read to you and don't breathe a word about it ... or it'll be the end of us. My cousin Marcel Nadjari wrote this note. He works in the crematorium opposite us. It seems he saw me from the other side and recognized me. For a moment I heard his voice from a distance, cautiously calling me and then ... he threw this little letter. I picked it up and read it. Read it now for yourselves, one by one for what he says."

The girls passed it from one to the other, read it, and then it came into my hands ... and with my own eyes I read the following, written in Greek:

> Dear cousin Sarika,
>
> I saw you from a distance and recognized you. I imagine there are many Greek girls there, as I have many Greek men here with me.
>
> I want to inform all of you about something you must keep secret for a while. Know that in two or three days, here in the crematorium, we are preparing a revolt against the Germans. Ready yourselves and be careful, girls. Maybe we'll be fortunate enough to succeed, come and save you, and all get out of this hell.
>
> Marcel Nadjari

After everyone had read it, we quickly tore it up and stared at each other. We were moved, but at the same time upset. What unexpected news! What should we expect in two or three days? No one knew what to say. This warning of a rebellion inside the crematorium shook us up completely.

From being half-dead, we suddenly felt the spark of life springing up within us. Now there is some hope, we said! Who knows, maybe ... so let's wait two or three anxious days with hope.

The revolt betrayed

Full of anxiety, we waited for three days, but all during that time we didn't notice anything unusual. There was no indication of any rebellion — until the end of the week, when just as we began to lose every hope, we heard shots and machine-guns outside while working in the barrack. We tried to get out of the building, but it was impossible. Through the door and windows we saw the crematorium opposite spitting flames and smoke from top to bottom — not from the chimney as was usual. Then we saw the men of *Sonderkommando* who worked inside running out towards us.

At the same time, trucks and cars with armed Germans arrived near our courtyard. They immediately attacked the men of *Sonderkommando*, ruthlessly cutting them down. Incredible chaos! A situation so horrible, I will never forget it as long as I live.

Our *Kapos*, who were inside with us and very frightened also, told us not to leave our places. Outside — shouting, screaming, killing! We saw men falling one by one, ten-ten at a time like flies without any defense, things that frightened us terribly.

Suddenly, two or three prisoners burst into our barrack begging for help and imploring us girls to hide them someplace.... Soon armed officers followed them. They came in, furiously threatening us to reveal where the prisoners who had just come in were hiding. My heart was breaking. I can still see this scene before me — the terrified faces of those unfortunate people who had just hidden underneath our tables and who could not possibly get out of there alive because we had no means of protecting them.

Shooting into the air, into the piles of clothes, under our feet, underneath our tables, the officers unfortunately dragged them out, and with their hearts in their throats they were handed over to be killed outside our barrack.

After a while, everything suddenly stopped — the shooting and the killing — only the human moaning of their last breath could be heard outside from time to time.

They didn't harm any of the girls at all. Toward evening, German armed guards escorted all of us to the barrack next door to sleep. We spent the night, of course, lying awake trying to fathom the tragic situation outside.

Throughout the night, mass graves were dug and the countless corpses of the prisoners who dared rebel were collected. They threw them one on top of the other and covered them with blankets so we wouldn't see them on our way to the other barrack next morning going to work. Later though, the graves were doused with petrol and the corpses were burned on the spot before our eyes in our own yard.

The few prisoners of *Sonderkommando* who remained inside and didn't come out of the crematorium, as well as those who ran for their lives into the woods, were arrested. But the Germans kept them alive, as they needed hands to dig the graves, to carry and bury the corpses of their beloved friends and colleagues.

The revolt of the Greek Jews in the Auschwitz crematoria was betrayed even before it got started. And for days after the event, the Germans were very nervous. This unsuccessful rebellion by the men in the crematoria was, no doubt, costly for them. It was also said that Crematorium III suffered damage.

One day toward the end of October, specifically on the 25th of that month 1944, an Austrian officer, while visiting our barrack for the control, approached the place where we Greek girls were working. He came up to us very cautiously and in a low voice whispered: "You, little Greek girls, do you know something? Your Greece has been liberated."

Auschwitz

The news came to us so suddenly, we started shouting for joy. "Really? It's true?"

"Yes it's true. There are no Germans in your country anymore. It's free."

This news of his, about which there was no doubt, started us crying like small children. Liberated from the German yoke, we could just imagine the Greek patriots dancing in the streets!

"But what does it mean for us here?" After our first reaction, we became conscious of our tragic state that was worse than ever.

Two more months went by and we were still in the same situation: continuing to work surrounded by the crematoria whose flames were devouring thousands of Jews every day with scientific precision. The smell of their burned flesh choked our nostrils and even affected our breathing, as if their souls were passing through our very being, leaving their traces and marks on us. The burden grew heavier with every passing day: their voices, the flames, the ashes, even their transformed fat in the form of the soap we washed with, wounded our body every day and ate our flesh. It couldn't go on. It seemed human endurance was at its limit. You felt so full of rebellion that the only release was to throw yourself on the electrified wire and be liberated.

I had reached the depth of hopelessness. I was almost at the point of insanity again when I sensed a familiar voice nearby and it was that of my friend Dora who came now from very far away, and it shook me and rang in my ears.

"Courage, strength Berry dear," she said to me. "Now is the time to keep your morale high."

"How can I?" I shouted.

"Search! One possesses a reservoir full of strength. Seek it out stubbornly this very moment if you want to be saved. Search for it, you will find it inside you, it's there."

Every time I listened to her voice, it transmitted its steely strength to me. This strength now set me in motion — a motion that pushed toward a single-minded goal. I wanted very much to live. I didn't want to die. So I gradually learned to draw upon a particular energy, an inner strength so enormous, that it became my sole weapon to overpower all those demons surrounding me and threatening me.

The crematoria blown up

It was the beginning of January 1945, when it was learned one day that the transports had abruptly and completely stopped. They were saying that Crematorium III had broken down during the rebellion. It was reported that the Russians invaded Poland. That the front was very near us! It was rumored that the Germans were losing and starting to retreat, and that the crematoria had to be blown up as soon as possible so there would be no evidence of their crimes.

We heard these things continuously, but didn't believe our ears ... until one day, our guards led us girls to work just outside the crematoria. There the men of *Sonderkommando* were already blowing them up, using dynamite everywhere, and we could see pieces of the crematoria fly into the air one by one and fall back down to earth.

The Germans were in a terrible hurry. They shouted like mad, "*Schnell, Schnell arbeiten.* Not one piece is to remain standing. Everything must be levelled. Everything must be cleared, every trace has to disappear." (They didn't want the Russians to get wind of any of it, so no testimony could betray their satanic deeds.)

The few men of *Sonderkommando* with whom we worked side by side carrying stones, earth, etc., were not in a hurry except to tell us — in whispers, as if delirious — what they had been forced to do here at this place where they had been working. How they suffocated the people, how they burned them! "You Greek girls, if one day you get out of here alive ... you must tell it to the world."

"Look," they said, "here were their disrobing rooms. Look here ... at these. These are the furnaces!"

And while they were talking non-stop, dynamite was blowing up everything: the stones, the iron and mortar, the concrete, all their criminal installations, their furnaces, their inhumanity — all the barbarism of the Twentieth Century was blown to the four winds.

This work went on in a hurry day and night. We girls worked only during the day. Then one day, as if by a miracle, we saw the crematorium nearest us finally levelled to the ground. This is how the story of the Auschwitz-Birkenau-Brezinka crematoria ended.

A very small crematorium — the 5th — was forgotten, or more likely they did not have time to blow it up. It has been preserved to this day as an example. Thousands of people visit it every day to pay tribute to the 6,000,000 Jews who were murdered in the Holocaust at Auschwitz, other camps, and at various locations.

January 18 — evacuation of Auschwitz

The German officers and guards did not conceal anything from us any longer. They came and went like mad, telling us flatly that in a

Auschwitz

few days Auschwitz was to be evacuated. All prisoners, men and women, would be taken somewhere further away.

By word of mouth we learned that great hardship lay in store for us on the road. So we discussed among ourselves that if we were to endure the hard winter cold, we at least, the girls of *Kanada* who were still able to get clothes from the piles, should prepare accordingly by securing a supply of pullovers, strong walking shoes, etc.

We didn't work anymore ... just waited for orders and events to happen. Meanwhile, we searched among the piles of clothes, this time for ourselves, to find the most suitable things for our situation.

I still remember how I prepared and how I was dressed. Fortunately, I was quite slim, and apart from what I had already put on, I was able to wear still more clothes: two girdles one on top of the other, three pairs of socks, a thick pair of trousers, a bra, and a heavy sweater. [I remember it was a very pretty yellow on one side and brown on the other.] On top of all this I wore a blue satin overall — like a school pinafore — with a zipper and two pockets, plus two pairs of gloves, and a scarf to cover my head and ears.

In the piles, I also found a big metal case in which a small knife, a spoon and a fork was concealed. I grabbed them, thinking they might be useful. I felt optimistic at the time, for fortunately, I didn't know what was in store for me....

Searching in the piles of shoes, somewhere in the middle of everything, I noticed a pair of short black boots with laces. They had an excellent woolen lining, thick and warm inside. So as for shoes, I was very lucky because these nice warm boots played a very big role in my life and contributed to my survival. As soon as I saw them I grabbed them, tried them on, and they fit perfectly! They were slightly bigger than my size — precisely what I needed to walk comfortably. From that moment on, I never took them off my feet.

It was already the 18th of January. All of us were ready for departure. An officer we knew, the same officer who had told us about the liberation of Greece, came to put us in order, five-five to a row. After bread and other provisions were handed out for the road, he told us we would be leaving soon.

Suddenly he approached me and singled me out: "You, get out of the line, you're not leaving yet."

"Not leaving! I'm not staying here alone without my friends. You cannot separate me from my Greek girl friends."

"Please get out of the line and sit somewhere apart."

A Cry for Tomorrow 76859 ...

Strangely enough, he spoke quietly and calmly without ordering me, but I was terrified. What now and why me? Why is this stupid Austrian separating me from the others?

I panicked. After I got out of the line, I secretly slipped in again near my friends, unnoticed. "Girls, please cover me ... don't let this crazy Austrian see me again and pull me out of line, I can't bear it."

The officer persisted, came to find me and got me out again. This continued two or three more times.

Finally, as I sat there alone crying, who should appear in the distance but Gruber! He hadn't shown up for months.... How he happened to be there at that moment, I don't know.

When Mati saw him, she came over to me and said something that seemed to make sense: "Berry dear, don't cry. If I were you, I would go and ask Gruber to let you leave with us. If you ask him, I'm sure he won't refuse you."

In my desperation I realized I had no other choice. "Let me go and God will decide!" So I approached him crying and begging — imploring him to send me away with the other girls, telling him that I was not able to endure being here alone without my Greek company.

As soon as he saw me he looked me straight in the eye, and then, very concerned, he replied: "Are you sure you want to leave with them?"

"I'm certain. I want to join them. I don't know what's in store for me here and anyway, why should I stay alone without my friends? What will happen to me?"

"Then what can I say ... go, if this is what you want. Go and join the line where your friends are."

After that the Austrian officer didn't come back again to take me out of the line. At that moment, however, I unknowingly was choosing my own fate. All those who stayed, for one reason or another, either because they were seriously ill and unable to walk, or because they were hidden in the woods, or in a tree, or somewhere else were liberated a few days later by Russian troops. Their Calvary and odyssey ended there on January 27, 1945.

The Death March

Pawns of the Third Reich

Nestled inside my row of five among my Greek girl friends, we were readying to leave when an order came that halted us at the last moment. They said we had to change direction because the Russians had already blocked several roads and it was impossible to get through. Two to three groups of prisoners who had left the day before, returned, accompanied by guards with their dogs.

Running every which way in a frenzy, the officers were determined to find an available road by which they could send us to Germany. They didn't want the Russians to liberate us. Germany still needed slaves. Unfortunately, we were very unlucky, for an open road was found, down which they were able to flee Auschwitz with most everyone.

After a two or three hour march on foot, an interminable road opened in front of us that would lead us incredibly far – all the way to Germany. So from here on, a new Calvary began and of the thousands of prisoners who set out on the march, very few would survive, for the majority would die on the road.

Much has been written about this endless walk. Many writers and eyewitnesses correctly call this road of martyrdom, "The Death March."

On this Death March we walked in rows of five, and an armed guard with one or two dogs was stationed every three or four rows on each side for the entire length. It was impossible to escape or even change rows. The guards, young soldiers with pistols, machine-guns, and dogs at their heels, became our most ruthless dictators and clearly demonstrated they were not joking.

"Whoever, man or woman, can no longer walk shall be shot on the spot," they said. "No one shall stop for any reason. Only onward."

Thousands of Jewish prisoners met on that road. It was a terrifying spectacle. Dressed in rags, they were walking with bleeding feet on clogs or with feet wrapped with rags because they had no shoes. Every two or three minutes, someone fell half-dead in the

A Cry for Tomorrow 76859 ...

snow. At their first fall, the guards finished them off with one shot.

These were scenes one cannot possibly describe in words and give the full picture.

From time to time in this vast snowy landscape, my vision grew blurred with fatigue and my tongue hung out. The little bit of snow we secretly put in our mouths now and then, was a moment's forward thrust to keep our feet moving, because they, God forbid, must never stop. So my body, like a machine, obeyed the orders I gave it, and I pushed on ... pushed on, as long as I could.

For a moment, I heard Mary with whom I worked in *Kanada*, crying like a baby next to me. I don't know why I found it so strange. I remember daring to ask her why she was crying.

"Where are they taking us?" she asked, continuing to cry. "I feel lost here in this snow, in these wild mountains. I see no way out ... I'm frightened."

At that moment I became aware that my mind had completely escaped reality and had drifted off somewhere far away from that horrible environment. I was walking like a robot, as if I were not there. It seems I was able to adapt to every situation in a different manner.

I was back to my fantasies again, in my own world, when as in a dream, I heard a familiar voice calling my name. It was my cousin Gita, whom I hadn't seen since I left Block 27 at Birkenau months ago.

This meeting was truly a miracle for both of us, an incredible piece of good fortune. To find each other side by side there among thousands of people was just so unexpected. We kissed, we hugged, we cried from emotion right there in the middle of the road as we plodded on.

After a few minutes I noticed how awful she looked and how she was shivering. The first thing I did was give her some socks, gloves, etc., things I was wearing from Brezinka, so she could somewhat collect herself. Then we clasped hands and promised never to abandon each other — until death.

At that moment I felt a warm glow from the joy of finding her. At last I had someone of my own from home giving me the strength to go on, be it only a cousin two years younger than I. Looking into her eyes, I understood she was thinking much the same thoughts. From now on we would help each other.

Fatigue was becoming unbearable. We were hardly walking anymore, only dragging our feet. My movements became unsteady. As night approached, we couldn't see in front of us any longer, and

The Death March

when it became completely dark, we found ourselves beside a barn.

Pointing machine-guns at us, our guards ordered some of us to go inside, to lie down, and pass the night there. After it had filled, others remained outside and lay on the snow.

My cousin and I entered with others into what seemed a stable with piles of slippery straw under our feet. I collapsed in the middle of a haystack, just as I was. My body, heavy like iron, felt nailed to the warm straw. Immediately, my feet painfully begged to be freed from the boots that were stuck to my dreadfully swollen feet. I had to do something right away, nothing else mattered, just the taking off of my boots and the closing of my eyes to sleep to forget everything.

But how could I do that? If I were to take off my boots ... barefoot people would grab them. It was no laughing matter. I faced a huge dilemma. But finally, my feet were so tired I couldn't tolerate it any longer. Besides, these feet that I would need tomorrow and the days after had to rest. I had to free them.

Though it would be difficult, I decided to take off my boots one by one; tie them to each other by their laces; and tie both boots again around my waist one at a time. In this way, I was hoping they wouldn't free themselves from my body before morning when I would need them again. Then I stretched my legs, removing my socks for a little before putting them on again. In two minutes I fell deeply asleep until morning when our guards came and opened the doors. I was so deadly tired that although I have claustrophobia, I didn't notice that they had locked us inside.

As soon as I opened my eyes, my hands searched around my waist ... finding only the one boot. The other wasn't there! I was insane with fear. Now I'm finished, I said to myself. You can't continue such a march with just one shoe. Oh, Berry! Your life ends here, you die! Hopelessness engulfed me ... I didn't want to give up yet. No, I didn't want to die. I wanted my boot. I screamed! I shrieked! I cried. My eyes searched to see if it was on somebody else's foot. I searched in the straw.

The guards were shouting *"Schnell, Schnell,* get out on the road, everyone out, you derelicts!"

I cried, cried, *screamed!* I kept searching for my other boot....

Finally, as if by a miracle ... yes, for me it was the greatest miracle of all because at that moment I found it buried in the straw!

A few minutes later, beaten and shoved by the guards, my cousin and I were out again marching in the midst of the mass of humanity.

A Cry for Tomorrow 76859 ...

Unfortunately, we were pawns in a big paranoid game. Though retreating, the Germans were taking us Jews with them. Before we died we could still offer something to the Third Reich. So they dragged us for days from Auschwitz to Germany, indifferent to who would live and who would die.

It was only morning, but we were already exhausted from having walked for ten or twelve hours the previous day. The guards, always beside us, led us down a hill from where we could now see some towns and villages. At the entrance of each town were young children, ten or twelve year olds, dressed in military khaki and stripes, with whistles and caps. Pitchers in hand of hot beverages, they were serving various refreshments so the guards could quench their thirst and change shifts with others.

We wretched people asked them for a sip also. I remember well, how those small children answered us in the most repugnant manner: "Nothing for you, never, *verfluchte* ... *Schweinejuden* ... damn, Jew pigs."

All the people of the towns and villages were aware that thousands of Jewish prisoners were passing through their cities, but they only escorted their guards.

On our way, we saw beautiful houses. Yet that which impressed us the most were the inhabitants living inside. We, who had been interned for seven or eight months in the darkness of Auschwitz, now for the first time saw old people, women, small children, babies in their prams, behaving as if nothing was happening, neither war nor misfortune. They were leading normal lives in their houses with their families.

The second day was horrible. Shootings by the German guards became more frequent — one after the other. They killed those who were the most wretched and exhausted in the lines. Those who had no strength to take another step, themselves asked to die! They preferred the release of death to dragging their weakened feet. Thus, we became fewer and fewer. The dead lying here and there, were more than the living still standing.

With my cousin beside me, we gazed at each other to see if we were still alive. For a moment I heard her say: "I can't go on. I can't take it anymore. I'll ask the guard to kill me. To find peace is perhaps the better way."

"No Gita dear, please ... don't do this to me," I said to her. "Lean on me for a while. Try to take a few more steps, you'll make it. Please don't die." And I held her, held her desperately to keep her from

The Death March

dying, so I wouldn't be left alone.

Later, her turn came to help me. In this way our love for each other saved us — a love we grew up with as children. It united us more than ever in those utterly difficult moments of our lives.

Finally, we reached a large city. They told us that it was Prague, the capital of Czechoslovakia. What in hell were we doing in Prague? But there, however, a dramatic event took place I shall never forget.

From our small crowd, a young girl stood up and pointed to a window opposite. "That's my house!" she shouted with emotion. "Please girls, help me get out," she said crying. "If I am to die, let them kill me here by my house."

She was a tall, pretty girl who spoke in Yiddish. She had been in *Kanada* with us. A girlfriend of hers, somewhat older, heard her plea and instantly made the heroic decision to help her. Whispering, she took it upon herself to give orders to the rest of us.

"Whoever is wearing something extra, take it off and give it to her so we can hide her cross." Yes, they had painted a cross on our clothes, front and back, so that from a distance we could be recognized as prisoners and unable to escape from the line. That's why we had to cover her cross at all costs. So the *Kanada* girls each gave her something of theirs, if only a scarf to cover her and tidy her up.

"Don't anyone turn their head," we heard quietly in Yiddish again. Her friend kept watching the German guards: "Take a step forward ... go ahead ... yes ... now no, stop."

The silence was deafening. We waited to hear the shot, to see her executed there on the spot. We continued walking, walking on until we left there. Nothing was heard. Did the girl survive? Nobody knows. I saw her leave the line of prisoners though, and disappear into the narrow streets!

After a while we left Prague and again came out to fields and snow-covered mountains. It grew dark, but this time there was no shelter or barn. We had to spend the night outside in the open until daybreak. That night we kept our eyes wide open, afraid to close them lest we fall asleep. There was danger of freezing from the severe cold. Shivering until dawn, we remained sitting on dead bodies.

Finally, on the third day, we stopped near trains and trucks. I remember that in one of the last trucks there were round loaves of bread. As soon as Gita saw the bread, she jumped on the truck like a tiger. I still wonder today, where she found the strength!

I looked at her like an idiot unable to move even my hand. Quick as a flash, she grabbed two round loaves and instantly gave them to me. We took a blanket from someone who had died and didn't need it anymore, and got into one of the trucks, pushed as usual by the guards and dogs to get on quickly.

Naturally, the truck filled up with one squeezed on top of the other. Fortunately, ours was open above, so we curled up somewhere, one next to the other. When finally settled, we were half-dead from prostration and the cold.

The first thing we did was hide the two loaves under the blanket lest the starving girls on the truck, who hadn't had time to grab any, might take them. Then we stared at each other.... It was unbelievable, but true. We were still alive and side by side!

Without many words we decided to take turns hiding underneath the blanket to eat a little dry bread to gain some strength. So covered up under the blanket, we ate bit by bit as the truck kept moving in the direction of Ravensbruck, Germany.

I learned afterward that less than one third of the 16,000 prisoners on the Death March reached their destination. In the road, we left behind frozen corpses whose human limbs were torn to pieces by the wolves and wild animals that came down from the mountains at night to eat them.

Others were boarded onto locked trains where approximately 120 people to a wagon were packed like sardines and forgotten for several days like trapped mice. Few survived. One of my uncles, some cousins, and friends of theirs who did survive, told me how people died screaming and shrieking in those closed trains, like the insane.

One of those was Abraham Mevorah, son of a Kastorian rabbi and my primary school teacher. Every day for months he wrote down his experiences in the camp. He held on to his diary until the last moment when he went insane, forgotten inside the sealed wagon of the train, choking from suffocation.

Ravensbruck

It was already late afternoon, almost evening, when we arrived in Germany. We entered a large fenced camp, but this time the barbed wire was not electrically charged. Its name was Ravensbruck. Entering the immense yard, we immediately formed rows of five, and then they started counting us again and again as usual.

New crowds kept arriving, lining up in rows of fifty. With so many lines, I thought surely there would be some girl we knew. I had

The Death March

to search. I marked the spot where my cousin was for fear of losing her, left my row and walked in among the other rows of tired crowds and started calling: "Dora, Lena, Rita, Regina, Burona, Nina, Rachel...." But no answer came from anywhere. Everyone looked at me oddly, listening to those strange names. I went back to my row empty-handed. Shortly afterward, they put us in barracks with bunk beds for the night.

Both of us tried to discipline ourselves to eat very little of the two loaves of bread, always leaving something for later. I also remember that we never looked to see whether one was eating more than the other. The love we felt for each other in those moments was more than brotherly — it was unparalleled! I can still see my cousin's eyes constantly looking at me with true devotion. Attached like Siamese twins, one became the half-self of the other. We didn't want to lose one another.

The following day we found Mila and Nina near some of the bunks. They were mother and daughter. Mila was trying to persuade her daughter to eat something, to keep her alive. They were Yugoslavians and had arrived in the transport from Kastoria with us, but had become separated from the rest of the Kastorians.

Afterward we met another pair of cousins, Lena and Rita. Lena was my childhood friend, one of those six inseparables back in Kastoria. From what I remember, Lena and Rita had been together since the very first moment they arrived at the camp and never separated. It seems that somehow each of us found meaning in having a family member to lean on and sustain life. But it was rare chance that brought one close to find the other.

Within three days we had to leave again. Ravensbruck was only the central assembly point for prisoners who arrived alive from Poland. From there, groups were sent to various camps inside Germany.

Gita and I were in our row again, when an SS officer noticed me and maliciously wanted to separate us once and for all. But as many times as he took me out of line, I slipped back in again, until in the end he lost me. So back on a truck with many other people, we travelled side by side to Retsov where we arrived around midnight.

Retsov

It was dark of night when they took us down from the trucks. We had entered what looked like an empty military camp and were herded - three hundred to four hundred women — into a metal non-masonry barrack. Our German guards showed us the space with candles and flashlights, so we would quickly settle ourselves. Everybody hurried to find a small place on the floor to lay down to sleep and pass the night. During those moments, I noticed that in the place where I had been pushed, there was a long, narrow, wooden table with a few chairs around it.

I had a foreboding. I didn't know from what. But that's why, out of fear, I thought to myself it would be better not to lie down, but to sit on a chair with my hands on the table as a pillow. In that position I would feel safer! So I did, and after a while everyone was sleeping wherever they had settled. After some hours, I heard shouting and screaming that shook me up completely. I immediately opened my eyes and realized it was pitch dark. I closed them again ... opened them again — nothing. I thought I was buried in black tar. The yelling doubled from every direction. It was a feeling of utter blindness that I shall never forget.

People were walking in the dark and falling on top of each other. Hands, feet, heads, utter chaos. Fortunately, I was seated holding on to the chair and the table. I thought it better to stay put, or I'd be trampled on and suffocate. Not a spark of light could be seen anywhere. Abandoned by the guards in this absolute darkness, we couldn't see our noses. We couldn't find a door or a window anywhere. It lasted for hours, and during this time I held myself from screaming, so as not to go insane. I waited, waited, listening to my heart beating hard from my agony.

The shrieks of the others reached a high pitch. Then I heard the beating of chairs and wood against the metal wall! How they found them that moment, I don't know. Madness had seized all minds, and all together like in an insane asylum, with hands, with nails, with chairs, they frantically searched for some light. Finally, they broke through the metal wall, opened one hole, two holes, after which light immediately flooded in from outside. It was midday! Now I understood where I was. I looked around at flushed, angry red faces full of fear and horror. Somewhere I found Gita looking terrible. And I wasn't any better myself.

At last, very late in the afternoon, the Germans opened the locks and chains from outside. After a time, we went out into the yard to be counted in rows of five. They brought us the black slop — "coffee" — and a little bread, and much later the usual dirty soup.

We understood we would be staying in that barrack for some time. But even the Germans realized they had to at least leave the door open because the barrack didn't have any windows. It was a stable. For this reason, they placed two or three guards with their dogs at the open door to watch us, especially at night. After that, I remember I woke up two or three times every night and went near the door to be sure it was open, returning to lie down for an hour, only to go back again.

As a result, I developed a terrible case of claustrophobia that subsequently affected my life for a long time. Whenever I happened to be in a large hall, cinema, or the like, I had to sit in an aisle seat very near the door, in order to leave whenever I felt the need. Fortunately, I have now overcome this phobia, but I had to work very hard to convince myself that the danger of darkness was forever behind me.

Human nature

In Retsov, we were not working and the atmosphere was agitated as the German position was continuously deteriorating.

One day, they ordered the opening of the storehouses stocked with food and other small items to be distributed among us. They had us form a line so we each could take something. These were things the International Red Cross had sent for us, which the Germans had kept hidden for years. Now, I don't know why, but they decided to distribute a little of it.

I happened to be the first in line, without wishing to be. Those behind me were screaming and fighting to get ahead of each other, to take something first. On impulse, I started shouting with authority at the girls behind me — with the air of a leader.

"Silence," I said.... "Stop screaming! Join the line one behind the other, or nobody is going to get anything."

Mechanically, they all joined the line again, looking at me scared, waiting for my next decision. With the manner I had adopted, they thought I was some responsible *Kapo*, appointed to this job.

I looked around and saw everybody waiting for my orders, ready to obey me like animals. Spontaneously, I went inside where the cans and other things were.... No one objected. As I did so, everyone stepped aside and accepted my leadership.

Nobody knew who I was. Oh my, I said to myself, just shout a little louder here and you are feared and obeyed. My God, look how easy it is to become a dictator. So this is how Hitler rose to power so quickly — no doubt by shouting and ordering, on each occasion more and more.

Then I started distributing the things with my own hands. As I handed them out, a little at a time, I simultaneously shared a smile and a friendly pat on the back. They looked at me stupefied! They took the things and couldn't believe that in this camp there were sweet voices, smiles, and kindness.

I myself could not believe how strong a person can be, if he wishes; or how weak, if he doesn't have self-confidence. On that day I was given an opportunity to understand human nature better. By assuming leadership, I acquired the greatest experience of my life, though I was still a very young girl.

Thus it is: a man can be very strong — a dictator, an oppressor, or a good and just leader — or weak and submissive, the plaything of other men. A man is what he is convinced he is.

After a few days in Retsov, they needed girls to do some temporary work. I volunteered among the first, as I couldn't stand the confinement of the camp any longer. I wanted to get out to look around the area. So that morning, about eight or ten of us left the camp singing (under orders) a German military march.

Fortunately, no crematoria existed there. The snow was scanty, but the cold was penetrating as we traversed a forest and arrived at a large isolated three-storied house that was being used as a small factory.

We went in. Somehow they showed us what to do, but I don't remember exactly what it was because they took me outside right away. I had to continuously pull on a lever though I never knew what it was or why I was doing it. But the work was easy, apart from the fact that I was freezing.

Our guards would leave as soon as we arrived at the factory and return in the afternoon to take us back. Our supervisors were two German citizens, one about fifty years old and the other seventy — a short dwarfish man with very tiny sick-looking eyes. I think the factory was owned by both of them. The older man was kind to us, giving us portions of the soup they brought for lunch, saying it was homemade.

There was almost no work there for us to do, but we asked them to say they needed us. Either they felt sorry for us, or they did it to have an alibi, fearing a reversal of fortune, as the general situation in Germany was changing minute by minute. In any case, we were eating hot nourishing soup.

One day, a lovely Yugoslavian girl who was working with us, said that in a corner of the basement storeroom there were about twenty kilos of potatoes.

"Shall we go down," she asked me, "to steal three or four potatoes?"

The Death March

"Let's go," I said.

When I saw the potatoes I went mad with joy, but as soon as my hand touched them, I grew frightened and stepped back. I instinctively remembered what my grandfather and grandmother used to tell me: "Good girls don't steal. It's a great sin. God is watching us!" But was God only watching me this moment? Was he watching so many other sins being committed? Besides, the Germans stole everything from me!

In this way I excused myself at the time, persuading myself to take two or three potatoes, which I had every right to do, so as not to die. Even if I steal them, I thought, I'll surely still feel honest — at least more honest than all those who have inflicted such harm on me.

I worked there for about a month and a half, going back and forth between the camp and the small factory. Every day when we returned to the camp late in the afternoon, the rest of the girls would be waiting for us to tell them our news. We were the only ones who got out, supposedly for work.

My companions were always the Greek girls, as we spoke the same language. The girls of this group came from all parts of Greece. Among us was Annoula from Ioannina, whom I now see in Athens and talk about Retsov. It was she who reminded me of that place.

This is what she related to me one day in the camp: She said from the moment the Germans arrested her in Ioannina, she hid ten gold coins on herself, and despite the ten or eleven months of slavery, imprisonment, and dreadful hardships, nothing made her give them up or lose them. She was sure one day they could be used to save her life.

This made such an impression on me at the time, that I still remember it. I think she was the only prisoner who succeeded in doing so, and it was a real achievement. Because there in Birkenau, with one gold coin, she was able to buy bread from time to time from the *Blockobersten* who were stealing the portions of other prisoners. For example, one time she bought four loaves of bread along with two packets of margarine and ate them underneath the blankets, though others happened to be nearby. This bread helped her survive and she was confident she would survive to the very end.

Laughing, but very emotional, Annoula tells me now that in Retsov, her last gold coin didn't prove lucky. She had bought four loaves of bread from the *Blockobersten,* and gave one to my cousin, Gita. They tore a blanket in two and made bags in which they hid the bread. That night, my cousin came to sleep next to me as always, leaving Annoula with the two bags in her arms. As soon as the girls of our group noticed the bags of bread, they kept watch on her continuously. After unsuccessfully attacking her two or three times, they waited vigilantly all night for Annoula to fall asleep. Then they seized the bread and it was devoured immediately. This is how things stood. Everyone was rabid from hunger, and a morsel of bread at the time was a matter of life or death.

The most notorious thief of all was Madame Loucha (that's what we called her). She was a fifty to fifty-five year old woman who was stealing continuously like a wild animal. I remember she stole some underwear from me — a girdle I had taken from *Kanada* — and other small things. When I discovered what she had done, I was so upset, I became furious with her. The following day I found her wearing my clothes, but she wouldn't give them back no matter what. She was unmanageable, foul-mouthed and so aggressive nothing could restrain her.

Of the Greek group, two beautiful young sisters stood out who were delightful. One was called Stella, but I don't remember the name of the other. One day, to cheer myself up somewhat after the distress Madame Loucha caused me, I approached these two girls who treated me with sweetness and kindness. How pleasant it was talking to these wonderful girls. By contrast, it seemed Madame Loucha did not come from a good family.

"Tell me girls," I said to the two sisters, "what part of Greece are you from?"

"You tell us first, and then we will tell you."

"I'm from Kastoria ... and you?"

"What did you say? From Kastoria! We lived in Kastoria for almost eight months. Truly, what a beautiful lake your Kastoria has!"

"It's impossible for you to have lived in Kastoria. If you lived there eight months, as you say, being my age as you are, I would have seen you somewhere. Kastoria being a small provincial town, any stranger coming there, even for a few days is noticed by everyone. People talk to each other. They would say, 'Look, there's a stranger in town.' I never saw you anywhere. Are you mistaken perhaps?"

"Even so," they insisted, "we lived in Kastoria."

"Where did you stay in Kastoria?" I asked.

"Up on the mountain above the bus station near Apozari. From our place we could see the beautiful lake every night like a mirror ... Are you convinced now?" Then they looked at each other and smiled.

"It's not possible," I told them. "Nobody lives there. As far as I know, there's only a house of ill repute up there. The Brothel of Kastoria. As you can imagine, we good girls were not allowed even to look in that direction."

"Eh, well, you hit the nail on the head, Berry. We worked in there, the both of us, in this ... house of ill repute as you call it."

"What! You?" I was speechless. I stared at them, stared at them again, unable to believe my ears.

"But you appear to be such good girls, maybe the best of all of us! How could you possibly fall in there?"

"Don't ask too many questions. Be assured that we continue to be good girls, that is, nice people. The two things are unrelated. Besides, all of us are illegal now."

"Truly, you and I and all of us here are of one category: We are Jews. Nothing else."

They were reasonable girls, quiet, and to be honest, I preferred them to the others. Why should I be concerned at such a moment what they were in the past? Besides, they have every right to dispose of themselves as they like, provided they don't bother or harm anybody else. And they, let God be my witness, neither stole from nor bothered or insulted any of us. We accepted them as equals and integral members of our Greek group.

Sometimes, when they were in a good mood, each in turn wanted to tell some things about their previous life. They talked very seriously about their experiences in the brothel. And all of us, with eyes and ears wide open, were entertained as if we were watching a movie.

When we finally arrived in Thessaloniki after our liberation, I met them both at the Jewish Community Center where we would all gather. But soon after, I lost track of them. They completely disappeared in Greece somewhere and I never heard anything about them again.

The general situation was rapidly changing. All the camp authorities — SS men and women — were very nervous. They were primarily concerned about themselves, then about their families, and finally about their country, which was slowly but surely going to rack and ruin.

The Russian and American allies were tightening their grip over Germany from all sides. With every passing day, the Germans grew weaker, and from being on the offensive, they were now on the defensive in their own country. So the turning of the tide was progressing at a rapid pace, and only barely and with difficulty could they hold on a little longer.

The guards and the SS were coming and going armed with their dogs as if crazed. The camp atmosphere was electric, and as we watched them, we asked ourselves what our fate would be in the end, as we were still in their hands.

One day they took us to sweep and clean a small airport. There, inside a fortress, some military planes were hidden. After a short time, an alarm sounded and under threat all of us were obliged to go into the fortress-shelter and hide there without giving signs to the enemy. Then came the deluge....

British planes flying very low over us, dropped bombs like rain. Our joy was indescribable. For the first time after a whole year, we saw there was a force from outside, able to shake the Germans. Yes, bravo, we said, go ahead even if we ourselves are in danger.

When the alarm ended, we came out of the fortress and were forced to push the small planes completely inside. Their "enemy," — the Americans, Russians, and English — were hitting that target exactly. Then we returned dead tired from the morning's air raid, praying to ourselves for something earthshaking to happen.

Watching the Germans disintegrate day by day, our faces shone with joy and furtive hope. But our mood was very irritating to the Germans. They couldn't stand the fact that they, the Devil-god Masters, dictators of almost all Europe for so many years, would end up being the slaves of their slaves. This idea drove them crazy, and thus continuously incensed, they became even worse toward us.

One day, I recall, I lived through the worst experience of my life. I still remember my body, how it stiffened like an unbending piece of iron when I found myself down under two dogs tearing at me as two SS beat me mercilessly with whips. I had done absolutely nothing. My whole being revolted. I turned black and blue, but I didn't feel pain. Believe me, iron is very strong, it doesn't bend. My friends and Gita were wailing.

"Why are you crying?" I asked.

"They will kill you. Don't you see what they're doing to you?"

"But I don't feel any pain," I said. "Really, I don't feel pain."

Oh God, how strong man can be when he fervently wishes to live! What a revelation! We owe it to World War II for teaching us this, because that war gave us the war of nerves and the concentration camp.

The Death March

The daily awakening

Prisoners of the camp

The Death March

At the Aussenkommando with musical accompaniment

The camp "toilets"

The Death March

Sleeping quarters of the prisoners

A Cry for Tomorrow 76859...

Preparations used in the "experiments" of Mengele

Block 10, Mengele's "laboratory"

A Cry for Tomorrow 76859 ...

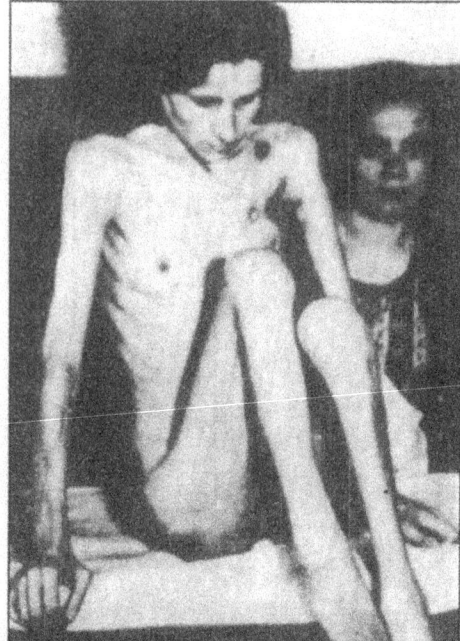

In the "Hospital"

The results of Mengele's experiments

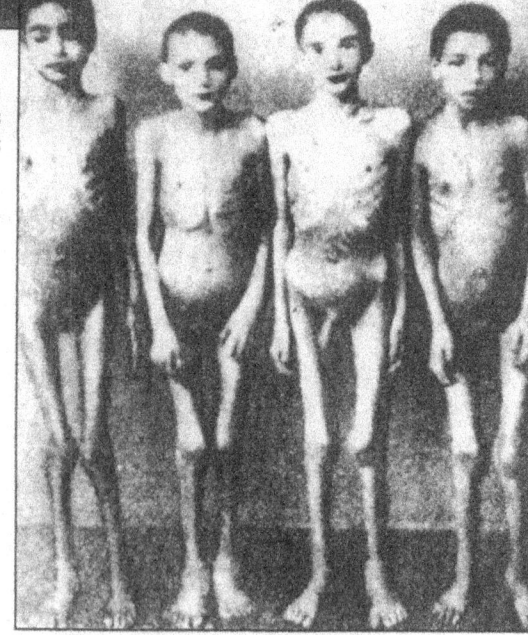

The Death March

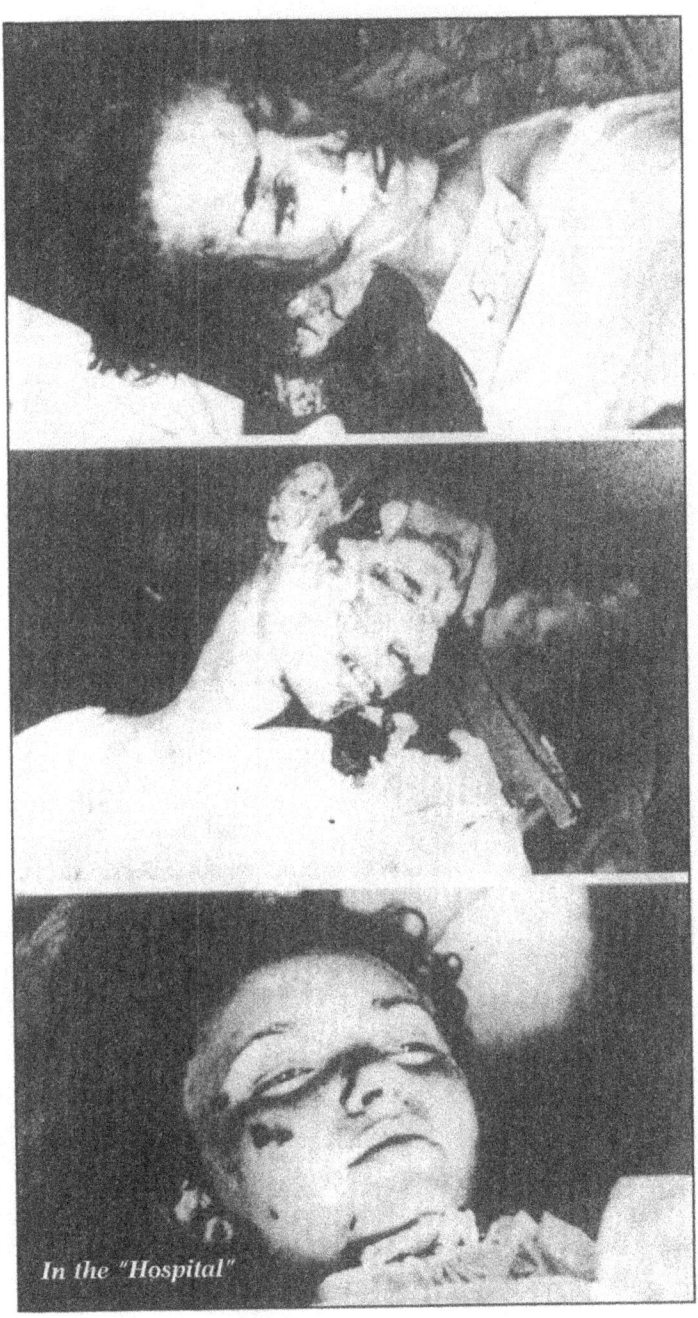

In the "Hospital"

Kanadakommando

The Death March

Zyklon B

The crematoria

Rudolf Hoess, the Commandant of Auschwitz

"The Final Solution"

The Death March

Frieda, Berry and Paula some months after their liberation

Toward Freedom

May 1, 1945

That morning which dawned was indescribable! What words, I wonder, am I able to find for such a circumstance? The words must be given life from inside me, exactly as I felt them at the time.

After the despondency of my past misfortune, how can I describe the intensity of my unexpected joy and the magnitude of my freedom? To do so, one must live those days again. They must unfold before you as if it were today ... and like today, to see them each again, to see them over again, to live them, to live them again as intensely as then.

It was the morning of May 1, 1945. As soon as we opened our eyes, we realized the camp gates were open! Yes, wide-open, and no guard was watching us anymore, nor was there a trace of a German boot. Nobody was with us. It was as if the earth had opened and swallowed them all at once.

Even the storerooms were open and the girls were going in and out of them opening the parcels that had been lying there so many years from the Red Cross. They untied them, chose things, grabbed things, took things, and quickly went out to the road one after the other with no escort anymore — incredulous, unable to grasp the reality.

Naturally, my cousin and I ran also, mixing in with the thousands of people whom we met in the middle of the road. Wagons, cars, motorcycles, push carts, all full of thrown together household goods, children crying next to their parents, men, women, young and old, running. Everyone came into the road from every direction. Holding hands, we joined in too, becoming one huge mob flowing like a stream, without ever looking back at the camp from which we fled, fearful lest we find ourselves back again in hell, in that cage. We shook the dust off our feet.

After some two or three kilometers, we found the courage to ask people in the crowd why they were leaving their homes, where they were going, and should we follow them.

A Cry for Tomorrow 76859 ...

"Behind us the Russians are approaching," we were told, "and in front of us the Americans are moving toward us. We prefer to join the Americans, that's why we're running toward them," the German people replied. In turn, they asked us who we were, why dressed in rags, why so weak and running. We told them we are Jews, prisoners with a number on our arm, and showed them.

"Oh, don't be afraid anymore, come with us, we will cover and protect you," they said.

After a while new people appeared on the same road — young Italian boys who had been war prisoners!

"Ragazze di dove siete? Parlate italiano?" Girls, where are you from? Do you speak Italian?

"Si, parlo italiano, ma sono greca." "Yes, I speak Italian, but I'm Greek," I replied.

"For your own sake, don't mix up with the German citizens. There are many Nazis hidden in their ranks so stay far away from them," the Italians told us. "All of us, prisoners and prisoners of war, should come together and form a separate group."

So we immediately left the German people and ran to follow our own kind. And the more we marched, the more people we gathered.

Suddenly my cousin said to me: "Why are we also running to reach the Americans? I don't care who liberates me. Why not the Russians ... is there a difference? Let's stop here, the Russians behind us will come sooner."

"No, Gita," I said. "Listen, if the Americans liberate us, there's a chance they might send us soon to America. We have relatives there as you know and could stay with them. But if the Russians liberate us, they may send us to Russia where we have nobody. So it's in our interest to run and be on the side of the Americans."

"I don't agree with you Berry. The thing I'm interested in at this moment is not to be interned as a slave in a camp. I only seek my freedom, and will be grateful to whoever gives it to me. So that's it. I'm not going anywhere. I'll wait here for the Russians."

Meanwhile it grew dark and in the distance we saw a little house like a barn on a hill. We went inside with several others to stay the night. The house being empty, we barely found anything to eat and slept on almost empty stomachs.

Very early the following day, we got up before daybreak and took to the road again with others. Without wishing to, we entered the streaming throng and walked wherever everyone was going. We didn't know what was happening because of the crush of people, and we could hear the gun fire of the front line. The war was now next to us! The situation was becoming more difficult by the hour and there was danger of our being killed by Russian shells from behind.

So we were on the run again, until we reached the opening of a forest. I remember it was getting dark when we stopped under a tree to rest.

"Now what will we do?" I asked Gita.

"We have no choice. We'll pass the night here on this rock under the tree," she replied.

"Yes, but what about the cannon fire? We'll be shattered, now at the last minute." "Oh, look, do you see here to the left of us," I said, "it's the gate of an old camp. Of course, there is the courtyard and the camp inside. What do you say? Shall we go inside to sleep for the night? And tomorrow we'll see how to start the day."

"Do you think I'm crazy enough to re-enter a camp again on my very own? Me! No, I'm not going in under any circumstance," she said.

"Don't be foolish. Can't you see that all the camps are abandoned? There are no guards anymore, nor a German uniform anywhere. Come, I'm sure it's smarter for two young girls to find shelter than be exposed outside to the dangerous front line of the war. Come," I said again, "please, look how many people like us are going inside."

I eventually convinced her and we went in. We immediately claimed a bunk and found a blanket as well. Exhausted, we fell deeply asleep until the following morning when the sun came up.

Just as we had bedded down in our clothes, we got up. Rested, we took a look out the window at the courtyard and then at the sun through the door we had entered the night before. Many people were outside. We heard shouting. There was great turmoil in the courtyard!

"What's going on now?" we asked the other girls. "And why are you shouting and crying?"

"German guards have blocked the door and won't let us out. We are prisoners again in a concentration camp!"

My cousin turned white and started to faint. "Oh, Berry, what did you do to me, what did you do to me? What did I tell you? What can we do now?"

I tore at my hair. My voice left me. I was barely able to utter a word. "Whatever you say to me, you are absolutely right. Even if you feel like killing me, do it."

A Cry for Tomorrow 76859 ...

All of us were crying at our new misfortune. We had just tasted a little freedom and they took it away from us again. Rather we handed it back, out of sheer stupidity. I couldn't comprehend it ... I couldn't bear such a thing anymore ... I didn't want to live.

Two hours passed. The cannon fire continued and was coming closer and closer. The guards at the door could not sustain their last gleam of power, for they suddenly abandoned it and miraculously disappeared, this time forever. It was the final madness of some Germans that thankfully lasted only one or two hours.

We went down, and there near the door, people were again pillaging the cans of the Red Cross. I had no strength for anything. I was overwhelmed by the latest incident, but my cousin plunged into the crowd like a wild animal. She grabbed two cans of food, gave them to me, and went back for more.

Finally, we deserted the camp and directed ourselves toward the forest. There were many of us, all prisoners and prisoners of war. We had to traverse a wood. These were the last hours on our way to freedom, and it would be a pity to get killed by the shells, the bullets, or the cannon fire continuously thrown by the Russians behind us.

A French prisoner of war assumed leadership. "Follow me," he said, "and do what I instruct you to do if you want to be saved, and for the sake of us all! Now fall on the ground," he said, "crawl to that tree. Don't anyone stand up so as to avoid the bullets."

Later, after having walked quite a distance, he ordered us to enter an abandoned two-storied German villa. When we were all inside, we were about eighty to one hundred people — those with the number on their arm and prisoners of war.

"Quickly, the women are to go to the upper floor and the men to stay on the ground floor. Search for a white sheet," our French leader continued. With a stick found somewhere, they made a white flag. Two or three war prisoners took the flag in their hands, climbed nimbly up on the roof and fastened it. The rest of us, closed in the villa, waited with great anxiety for events to unfold.

Suddenly, I asked somebody: "What is today's date?"

"It's May 4th 1945," he replied.

Very moved, I remembered that on that day, a year and a half ago, six of us girlfriends in Kastoria fixed a meeting for May 4th of 1945 — to meet, we said, all together no matter what in our Kastoria. And I asked myself, "Who else is still alive today?"

Toward Freedom

Liberation by the Russians

The area where we were was called Malhov, so it was in Malhov that we waited for the final miracle. At twelve o'clock midnight there was a knock on the door of the villa. Some of the men rushed to open it, holding a list of all our names and arm numbers.

Waiting with our hearts in our throats, we were extremely anxious to see what would happen. Armed Russian soldiers were asking us to tell them what was going on inside and why we had raised a white flag on the roof.

I don't know how they explained it, but our men told them that we were eighty to one hundred prisoners from various German camps, and that we were waiting for the Russian army to liberate us. The soldiers requested that seven or eight of our men go immediately with them to their superior and get food for at least three days for us.

"We advise you that nobody go out of here for a period of three days. Be careful, it is dangerous because the front line of the army is passing through. War is still being waged out there," they told us.

They brought us bread and various foodstuffs, even chicken from the next villa. Meanwhile, two or three armed Russian soldiers were placed as guards at the door to protect us from the danger of the passing army.

During these three days we became very close to each other, as if we had been friends and acquaintances for many years. We were from all parts of Europe, some from France, others from Italy, from Greece. All fellow prisoners, comrades in the hardships and the great moment we were waiting for — our freedom!

Freedom is a great feeling. It is something I cannot express in simple words... unless I evoke this great historic moment and live it again as intensely as on the fifth of May 1945, the day of our resurrection! But this is about how we all felt: an immense, ineffable joy. And for the first time we cried, hugging each other from emotion for at last the door of the villa opened!

They told us we could come out and go to an old camp somewhere on our left where a temporary military hospital had already been set up with Russian doctors and nurses to provide first aid. Each one was to immediately give the address of his home and his country of origin, and in a few days, they said, repatriation would begin! "You are going home." Was this dream or reality?

I was so immensely moved that my feet did not obey me. "How weak I am in this our great moment," I said to my cousin. "I have no strength. I don't know what's wrong, but I don't feel well."

"Nothing is wrong with you. Don't be afraid anymore. Go to the place they told us about, ask for an aspirin and you will feel better ... you'll see."

"Yes, you're right. I'll go. Where will you be?"

"I'll wait for you here outside," she said.

So I went into the improvised hospital. Inside the doctors and nurses took care of me immediately. First they took my temperature. My head was hot and my eyes red. As soon as I saw the Russian doctors, something strange happened to me ... I abandoned myself and gave over into their hands. I didn't want to react anymore. Enough, I said.

"Well, you have a fever of 103. You can't leave, you must stay here. But we are going to cure you," the doctors told me.

"You can't keep me here. I'm free now," I said, shivering from the fever. "Am I not? Tell me, am I not free?" I asked again.

"Of course you are free, but here you will recover so you can go home."

They wouldn't let me move.

"Please let me at least inform my cousin. She's waiting outside for me."

With the nurses accompanying me, I got up feeling like a wet rag, hot with fever. I told Gita through an open window that I was sick and had to stay there. "They won't let me go. I can't do otherwise." We both cried because we were going to be separated.

"Tomorrow we are leaving. They told us they're taking us someplace else. How can I leave you?" she said to me.

"Don't be concerned about me," I said to her. "Tell any relatives you may meet from now on, that you left me here alive. If I recover, we'll rendezvous in Greece. In our Kastoria!"

I blew her a warm kiss and neither of us knew if we would meet again.

There we separated.

Typhus

I stayed in the military hospital for a long time. There I lost all sense of feeling, even the sense of time. For days and days I wasted away from fever and flickered between life and death. The only thing I do remember, as in a dream, are the cold wet sheets in which the doctors continuously wrapped my naked body, no doubt to bring down the fever. There were no antibiotics in those days. They hadn't been discovered yet.

After some time, I don't know how long it was, I was able to perceive a smile. "Are you feeling better?" the doctor asked me. "You had typhus, you know, but you are out of danger now. Don't be afraid anymore."

A long period of convalescence followed. The food they started me on was a small portion of the same camp soup with potato peels and the same nasty look. I thought I would lose my mind.

"Why? Where am I," I asked them. "Am I in a camp again? And how can you possibly save me? Tell me, are you not my saviours? And since you have liberated me, and since you have cured me of typhus, why are you giving me the same camp soup again?"

"Because your organism cannot digest anything but this soup," they explained to me with kindness. "Trust us ... little by little we are going to add something more to this soup. Don't be afraid."

Indeed, after a few days they added a little potato, then a little meat, and in a few days the soup became a normal soup with rich ingredients. Soon I reached the point of eating as much food and bread as I wanted. Many who survived to see the days of freedom, died because they ate fresh butter and American chocolates.

With the passage of time, I felt better. Then one day they told me that I had to leave there. "You are going to another building not far from here, where people aren't seriously ill. There are other girls like you there who are waiting to completely recover and go home."

The following day they transported me in an ambulance to a convalescence center. As soon as they took me inside, I heard Greek and Spanish in Thessalonikian dialect! Wonderful, I said to myself, by all means I'll be with Greek girls here.

The nurses put me in a room with an empty bed next to three or four beds occupied by other girls, and left. After a while, I heard Greek being spoken again very loudly in the room next to mine. This time I shouted as loud as I could. "Any Greek girl out there, please come to my room!"

Lo and behold, a thin girl with big black eyes arrived limping. As soon as she came in she asked: "Who's the Greek girl here?

"Me," I answered. "What's your name?

"My name is Paula and I'm from Thessaloniki. A Frieda is here also and she's Thessalonikian too. Here she is!" And just then another girl came in, a bit tall, with large round eyes and a beautiful smile....

A Cry for Tomorrow 76859 ...

So this was Frieda. Their smiles and our acquaintance cheered me up and it was very good for me. Soon, of course, we started telling each other our personal odysseys.

Paula and Frieda said they too were Auschwitz prisoners with numbers on their arms, but we never met during all the time of our incarceration. Each of us had apparently worked in different places. We became friends immediately, helping one another, for we had to completely recover in order to return to Greece, our *Patrida*, our Homeland. That is what we called it.

Soon they brought us another Greek girl, very sweet, with dimples in her cheeks. She was of average height but very weak, and her feet barely supported her.

"What's your name?" I asked her.

"Sarika Venezia. My husband was Hugo Venezia and I heard from friends that he was working in the crematorium, in *Sonderkommando*. Do you know anything of him?"

"Yes," I replied, "that is to say I think he worked opposite the place where I worked in *Kanada*. I have the impression that the last people who worked there were saved." (Yet I was sure he was killed in the rebellion.)

"I hope so," Sarika said to me warmly. "Do you think I'll be lucky enough to see him again? We loved each other very much."

Sarika proposed the idea to snitch two or three sheets and sew some underwear, as we didn't have any. "We must prepare for the return journey," she said with emotion. "I know how to cut, and you can sew them by hand. Do you agree?"

Very quickly we organized ourselves, found white thread, scissors, needles, and laid out our sewing. Sarika's hands were shaking badly, but the poor girl tried to help us all, despite her weak condition.

Every day the nurses came by to take our temperature. One day Sarika had a high fever. They took her from my room at once with the presumption that she would be back soon ... but Sarika never returned to us. If she had recovered, by all means they would have brought her back. Poor thing, she wanted so much to return to her homeland with us.

Lice

In the convalescence center we were three Greek girls — Paula, Frieda and I — among Polish, Czechoslovakian, Italian, Yugoslavian, and other girls from almost all over Europe. After a short time, we realized we all had itching heads, and it was announced that the center was full of lice.

All during my time as a prisoner, I don't remember ever having a case of lice. Perhaps it was because I worked in *Kanada*. But now, every morning we had to wash our hair and examine each others' head. We laughed with the naiveté of youth, and occupied ourselves all day by picking out lice, baby lice, and the tiny eggs stuck on every single hair. Apparently they proliferate very rapidly.

One day Paula found an ivory comb that belonged to the Polish girl who slept next to her. The comb made the rounds of the girls from head to head. As I recall, it was an old comb with very dense teeth on both sides and quite miraculous. Getting down on our knees, we applied the ointment, "Mitigal", morning, noon and night, and slowly, with great patience, a little laughter, and a few tears, we completely removed the lice from our hair.

I'm not ashamed to say that the ivory comb finally ended up with us, the three Greek girls. We stole it, hid it, and said it was lost. "Greco theft!" We decided it was an item of necessity that we must have with us for every eventuality.

The typhus we suffered caused our hair to begin falling out and now the medicine we applied worsened the sparse condition of hair on our heads. But we were alive and feeling better. That was the most important thing for us. Only Paula was complaining that her legs ached, and bending her knees was difficult. Still, she was enthusiastic, outgoing, and very good-hearted.

The waltz contest

The place of my liberation, the convalescent camp at Malhov, became our residence. They were not going to transfer us anywhere else, for we had almost entirely recovered. We ate, drank, and slept there, and were free to come and go outside or receive visitors from other blocks where all sorts of ex-prisoners were staying. Very rarely did we need medical care, but whenever it was needed, there were doctors and a hospital at our disposal.

As time went by, we discovered new feelings. At last we felt like normal human beings again, with rights and obligations as before. This gave us the motivation to start a new life with joy. Slowly but steadily, we were awakening from the long lethargy of yesterday with its bad dream and nightmare. Now, we said, we must close all those things in a drawer, lock them up inside us for as long as necessary, until we recover psychologically. Hopefully that would happen quickly. Thus, being born anew, we could inaugurate a new future because we were still very young and a long life was opening before us.

One day I unexpectedly found a black ivory bracelet somewhere. It was beautiful and had the following French words inscribed on it in blue: *"Dieu vous protégé,"* "May God protect you." I took it as a sign and put it on immediately. I never took it off my wrist thinking I was very lucky, for Providence, if she exists, sent it to me today. I felt a sense of optimism and smiled. And besides, this was my first piece of jewelry after my imprisonment!

One afternoon we went out into the countryside, and nearby on a race track young men and women were singing and dancing. They had even organized a dance competition. A handsome young man came over as soon as he saw me and asked me to dance. My heart skipped a beat and I remembered how well I used to dance in my Kastoria! But I hesitated and asked myself ... should good girls dance with strangers?

As if he understood my thoughts, he said to me, "Look, here we are all brothers. We are all alike. We must celebrate our liberation. Just think how lucky we are to have survived."

Of course. He was right.... Yes, why not! And I set myself free, whirling to the beautiful sounds and music of the waltz. It was the first dance of my deliverance. My feet moved nimbly and my caballero was a very good dancer, lifting me like a feather in the air. I couldn't believe it myself.

Little by little the others dropped out as they grew tired, and at the end, three couples were competing for first prize.

"Don't show weakness," my caballero told me. "You dance wonderfully. We shall win, you'll see. Everyone is looking at us."

Indeed, we were the last dancers and as we finished, all the young people came around to congratulate us and give us first prize for the "waltz." I thanked my caballero and he did the same with great enthusiasm. I asked neither his name nor where he was from. It didn't matter, he was an ex-prisoner like me and, of course, I never saw him again. Even now, however, I fondly remember how courteous he was to ask and persuade me to dance with him!

The flirt

One day Frieda came in, boisterous and joyful. "Girls, I found caballeros — flirts for all three of us! They are three very good-looking young Italian men. Nice boys, educated and polite. I know what I'm telling you. You are very young, but I'm not mistaken in such matters."

"Well," Frieda went on, "I have already chosen Giuseppe for myself. I like him a lot. Besides, I saw them first.... You, Berry will take the second, [I don't remember his name ... let's call him Sergio] and the third, the rather slim slightly tall fellow you'll take, Paula."

"All right," Paula said, "but let's see them first."

I was furious with Frieda who rushed to find a flirt for me and moreover, chooses him and imposes him on me! These things happen spontaneously, they can't be prearranged. Furthermore, (talking to myself, without betraying my thoughts) is it proper to flirt here, far away from home? What if the flirt abandons you with child? Another Calvary after having just suffered Auschwitz. So I said to myself, Berry, don't do crazy things. Your father always said: "Your future depends on you. Be careful what you decide and what you choose. Be responsible for yourself and for your actions."

While I was having these thoughts, Frieda said to me: "So, what are you afraid of? These fellows won't harm us. We can at least let them come to meet us."

"Let them come!" I said. "But tell me something Frieda, did this Giuseppe tell you he wanted you?"

"Not yet, but he will."

The following day the three young men arrived like bridegrooms. Frieda took the introductions upon herself in French, which she spoke fluently: "This is Giuseppe Lucarelli, and this is Sergio, and this is [the other fellow's name]. My friends, Berry and Paula."

I extended my hand to all, and replied in Italian.

"Molto piacere." (Nice to meet you.)

"Ah!" Giuseppe said, "I see you know Italian. *Bravo!*"

"Yes," I answered and spontaneously looked at him and saw how attractive he was! Dark complected with intelligent blue eyes. Frieda was right, I thought. He was a rare type. Naturally, because he impressed me, I stared at him awhile. He caught on immediately. From that moment, Giuseppe didn't leave my side despite the fact that all the while I tried to make general conversation without showing preference to any of them.

Giuseppe abruptly interrupted and said to me: "Berry, would you come out for a moment please? I want to tell you something privately." I accompanied him to the door and there, unexpectedly, he seized my hand and kissed it. "Good-night Berry," he said to me. "I'll come to see you again tomorrow."

A Cry for Tomorrow 76859 ...

Thus, without understanding how, Giuseppe became my flirt and Frieda was obliged to take the one she had intended for me!

At Malhov, repatriation began and groups of Slovak and Polish girls gradually bid us farewell and left for their homes. "Look, it's very easy," they told us. "We wrote all our names down on a list and informed our country that we are here. Poland and Czechoslovakia responded immediately, and in a few days a bus will come to pick us up. Moreover, we are close by."

"What will happen to us?" I said to Paula and Frieda. "Who in Greece is going to be interested in us? I don't think anybody. No one will come to take the three of us from here, being so far away as we are. There's only one way," I said. "We must leave Malhov and go to Berlin as soon as possible. Upon arrival, if there is a Greek embassy, we shall present ourselves to them personally."

Giuseppe said the same thing to himself and to his Italian friends: "We few Italians have more or less the same problem." Two or three Yugoslavian girls whom we knew also said the same thing.

But I saw that none of them was making a decision, and because my mind continually thought about this situation, I came up with a brilliant idea. I gathered the Yugoslavian girls, the Italians, and the other two Greek girls and had a meeting. "I propose," I said, "because our countries neighbor each other, we form one group and leave together. We Greeks don't mind if they take us to Italy or to Yugoslavia. From either of these countries it will be easier for us to go Greece."

Everyone agreed to leave together, but they asked by what means.

"Tomorrow," I said, "I'll go and speak to our Russian area commander, announce our joint decision and ask for his help."

Indeed, the following day I conversed with the commander through an interpreter. He was a kind man who was moved the moment he saw the tattoo on my arm, and listened to my tragic story of the crematoria in Auschwitz.

"I must tell you that the road is dangerous," he said. "First, as soon as they see you, they will force you to work repairing the railway lines. "Second, you girls will be in danger. But I think I can help you with a safe way. I will give you two official stamped papers that you will always carry on you. The one will be an order from me, and you will show it to every mayor or authority of the city through which you pass. This will be valid until you reach Greece. Whoever reads my order is obliged to provide every assistance you need, including food and shelter until the next town. And the other paper will say the following: 'The girls of this group suffer from a contagious fatal disease.' So if you think you are in danger of being forced to work, show it and nobody will bother you. They will all run away."

"Is there any possibility you can send us by safer means?" I asked him.

"For the time being, no," he replied, "unless you wait three or four months more, until all the railway lines destroyed by the war are repaired. There is no normal road yet."

I was moved in turn by the kindness of this man, and I told him that I would never forget what he did for me as long as I live. I thanked him very much, took the papers in my hand, and left.

The road of return

In two days our small group — three Yugoslavians (two women and a man), two Italians, and we three Greek girls — was ready for departure. Psychologically, we were prepared to face all the obstacles the Russian commander of Malhov pointed out to me and which I, in turn, explained to everybody. The first problem was Paula, who was physically unable to walk very much. Her legs were almost bent over. After a few steps, she had to rest.

"Don't worry Paula," I told her, "you're okay just as you are, and I promise I'll take you all the way to our Greece. Trust me and lean on me. Come, give me one of your hands and slowly let's leave Malhov. We'll make it together."

With our rucksacks in our hands, with the papers of the Russian commander hidden on me, with the assistance of Giuseppe always by my side, I assumed leadership with great optimism.

Giuseppe Lucarelli was an excellent young man, twenty-three years old, a civil engineer, intelligent, and a good friend with a lot of understanding and respect for all of us. He also had war experience. A little before the Germans took him as a war prisoner, he lost half his thumb in battle. I can say that without him, we at least, would never have reached our destination.

In the beginning, we decided to walk for a time on the motorway until we found some help. Indeed, after hitchhiking a while we stopped a truck, the back of which was the open kind with two benches, one opposite the other with other people sitting there. The driver asked us where we were heading. We told him.

"Your destination's Berlin, but I'm not going that far. If you want, get up, and I'll take you to the next village and from there find other means."

A Cry for Tomorrow 76859 ...

This is what we did. After settling down in the back of the truck, I urged everyone to sing. "We're going back home," I said. "Let's all begin courageously with a song."

Our youth, our thirst for a new life, my self-confidence, and the trust everybody showed me, made me feel optimistic and at the same time responsible. I was sure we would make it and overcome all the obstacles we would meet on the long road ahead of us.

After two or three hours, the driver let us off at the next village. There, because of Paula's weakness since she couldn't walk very much, I suggested we stop someplace so as not to tire her. They agreed to sit somewhere and keep Paula company.

"All right, fine" I said, "With the papers I have, I'll go find the authorities of this place to give us food and shelter. As soon as I'm finished, I'll immediately come to meet you here where you're sitting."

Giuseppe, of course, came with me. The fact is I needed a male escort. The environment was unfamiliar; the situation difficult.

Having finally found the mayor of the town (by then I could speak German quite well), I gave him my paper, and as soon as he read it, he readily gave plenty of coupons for everyone to eat for two or three days at a small restaurant. He also gave us a note by which we could request hotel accommodations for at least two or three nights.

With much joy, I had verification that the papers of the Russian commander were *passe-partout* for us. And once we learned where the small restaurant was, Giuseppe and I ran to bring the whole company there.

First, we helped Paula, step by little step, and after a time we were all gathered at the restaurant-tavern. Such as it was! Going in, we had to wait in line because many people were ahead of us. After a while, with coupons in hand, they gave us a table. Potatoes with meat and lots of bread were served, some of which we took with us.

From there, we headed for the hotel where we found a very unpleasant surprise. The hotel did not have rooms, only large halls for foreigners like us who needed shelter. This meant everyone had to sleep together on the floor, topsy-turvy. Furthermore, as soon as we got in and saw the situation, I didn't like it at all. Most of the guests were men, who as soon as they saw us, began staring and scrutinizing us girls.

Despite the fact that I was next to Giuseppe, a man speaking Russian came by and made a fresh pass at me. I was frightened because I understood he had bad intentions. First he went to move Giuseppe out of the way ... but I noticed it immediately and before he had time to make another move, I managed to stick the Russian commander's second paper in his face. Perplexed and wondering why, he read the paper through with curiosity.

"Ahh! Ahh!" he shouted like a mad man, throwing my paper down and running off. Then he began shouting to the other men in a language I didn't understand. Apparently he explained to them what he had read: that we women had a contagious and fatal disease. Panic ensued throughout the hotel.

"Grab one blanket each and go downstairs quickly," I said. "It's impossible to stay here overnight. Moreover, we women are in danger." In a few minutes all were down and we left the vicinity of the hotel as quickly as possible. "Everyone follow me." I told them. "We'll go to the railway station and wait for the train."

By asking, we eventually arrived and found many people like us, curled up here and there opposite the station.

"Bring your blankets, spread two down here and leave one or two as a cover. The men will lie down at the corners; the women will go to the middle." I took a place between Paula, who needed support, and Frieda. Then the others followed. "All the women should cover their heads with the blanket. The men can leave their heads out." Fortunately it was almost summer.

This is how we settled ourselves that first night under the railway station, directly opposite the trains. Nobody bothered us. At daybreak next morning, as soon as we opened our eyes, luck was with us for a train came to take on people and it was going in the right direction.

In the train

It was an old train we had boarded, and was headed toward Berlin. They told us it would make many stops along the way, so at the first stop, we got off with others in a beautiful small town though I don't remember its name. We had not changed our chartered course, but we had to stop at times because of Paula. Giuseppe and I went to the town authorities, showed my paper, and were given coupons, bread, and other things.

One day Frieda made a nasty observation which upset me a lot. She said I shouldn't be as fair and just with everybody else by dividing the food equally. "Why do you do that?" she said. "We count first, your two Greek girl friends. We should eat better and more. You shouldn't consider everybody the same. You run and tire yourself more than anyone, and the others, what do they do? They wait for you to bring them their food and spoon feed them."

"But that's not right, Frieda dear," I told her. "Either we are one company, or we're not. We must all eat alike."

"No, I don't agree with you," she insisted. "You're ridiculous...."

"You're right." I said to her, and immediately conceived a plan to teach her a good lesson.

The next time I went with Giuseppe to find food as usual. That day, they didn't give us coupons for food. There was no restaurant in that town. They only gave us coupons to get some bread from a bakery and nothing else, so we took four warm white loaves. Right away I said to Giuseppe: "Do me a favor. Tell our friends that we didn't find food anywhere (which we didn't), but tell them as well that an Italian friend whom you met by chance gave you these four loaves. Then, take the bread and share it equally among everyone, as if it were yours. Understand?"

Giuseppe understood something, but I obliged him to do what I said without much explanation. I urged him not to say anything to anyone.

As soon as we got back to the company, I immediately announced to my Greek girls in Greek: "Unfortunately, today they gave us neither food nor bread. There are no coupons and no restaurants operating here. These loaves of bread belong to Giuseppe; they're not ours. Don't any of you dare ask for any. He alone will give us some, if he wishes to. An Italian friend whom he happened to meet by chance at a bakery, gave them to him," I said.

Frieda approached Giuseppe, swaying her hips, saying to him: "Eh, Giuseppe, you're a nice guy, aren't you?"

"Of course," he replied, "I don't plan to eat all four loaves myself even though a friend of mine gave them to me. I'm going to divide them equally as we always do."

Frieda didn't utter a word, just took her appropriate share and thanked Giuseppe very much. I hoped she understood for good that we constituted an inseparable group, irrespective of religion and country, and that we must stay together, love each other, and enjoy equal rights and obligations throughout our journey. Indeed, from then on, there was no other discussion about unequal sharing.

My cousin again

One day as we were just walking around in another town, they told me that high up on the hill was a free camp full of girls like us, waiting to be repatriated. I was very curious and wanted to go up and see who they were. I left the group below and climbed way up to the top on foot with Giuseppe. The first person I met was my cousin Gita!

Our feelings were overwhelming! We kissed, embraced, cried that we had met again after so long, and seeing me really alive standing before her was unbelievable.

"Who is he?" she asked me in Greek.

"He's a friend, a very good friend.... He's Italian."

She hardly greeted him, not liking the fact that I was being accompanied by a man.

"If you wish, you can stay with us, there are many girls here whom you know. Stay and we'll leave together," she said to me.

"When are you leaving from here?"

"It's not known yet," she answered. "Here one needs a lot of patience with these Russians, and for the time being, I can't say until the trains and tracks are repaired."

"To tell you the truth, I don't have much patience, and besides I can't stay as I'm part of a group who is waiting for me down in the town. We are independent and free. We have papers and many other kinds of assistance. Everything is in order for us to continue on. I can't stand this place any longer, Gita dear, and moreover, if I leave them, they won't make it. They don't know German and we have a sick girl with us. I feel sorry for them. It's a shame, but impossible. They're all waiting for me. Believe me, I'm so happy seeing you again, yet very sorry to have to part with you. To our reunion in Greece, my dear.... Let's see, whoever arrives first will wait for the other. Okay?"

Very moved, we kissed each other and separated, hoping this time it wouldn't be for long. Then Giuseppe and I made our way down to the company we had left who were waiting below with bated breath until they saw us again.

Berlin

The following day we boarded another train, this time taking us direct to Berlin without another stop. During those two or three days we ate only bread and salt. There was nothing else anyone could give us. I was neither concerned, nor ever worried that I was undernourished.

Half stretched out in the old train, we left the door open to enjoy the train's rapid movement that this time would take us to our destination. Toward evening the train shook once or twice and blew its whistle loudly announcing that we finally arrived and could get off.

Berlin was ghastly, horrible, almost completely destroyed by

A Cry for Tomorrow 76859 ...

the bombings. It was the first months after the war and the Berliners themselves had not managed to return yet. There were almost no people.

We crossed the Brandenburg Gate all together and saw a square where crowds of people like us with rucksacks and blankets were sleeping on the ground. I didn't like staying there even though it was well lit. So this time, I suggested to our group that we go back through the gate on foot the way we had come. I explained I had seen from the train the shells of several large houses destroyed by the bombings. "We'll go into one of those destroyed houses. At such an hour there's no possibility of finding a better place to pass the night." And so we did.

"The safest place of all is right here, I think. Let's take care, however, not to light a match or talk amongst ourselves so as not to attract anyone's attention. We'll settle on stones, two persons to a blanket, and if we manage to get some sleep before daybreak, so much the better." Everyone agreed.

So we passed the first night in Berlin wrapped in our blankets, sitting on stone and leaning by the gaping holes of former windows. The following day we entered the square again, where the company settled themselves temporarily. I told them to wait for me and that I wouldn't be long.

Asking our way, Giuseppe and I made it to the mayor. Using my German, I began the same story, showing the official paper of the Russian commander and the number on my arm. This time, the mayor was a very educated and cultivated man. As soon as he heard I was Greek, he began to recite Homer, speaking to me in ancient Greek and explaining the theories of Greek philosophers. He was very emotional and couldn't resist the opportunity to show off his knowledge. I wasn't very enthusiastic because I was impatient to tell him other things that were on my mind, but I restrained myself.

I was impressed, of course, by how educated these Germans were, but didn't anyone have anything to say about the war? Anyway, in this instance, the mayor of Berlin did everything he possibly could to help. I was given coupons and many other things, and the more I thanked him, the more interest he showed. He escorted us to the door and said that he would be very glad to see us again if we needed him and would always be at our disposal.

With the coupons in hand like a treasure, we went straight to get bread. Everyone was hungry and waiting for us to return laden with mana from heaven.

On the way we heard Italians talking to one another. Even though we were hurrying, we began talking to them to gain information. Very briefly, they told us they were staying high up on the hill at a large camp and coming regularly to Berlin by tram. The place was only twenty minutes away, they said. "We stay in barrack like lodgings and are under Russian supervision. We are fed generously and what's more, are free to come to Berlin whenever we wish."

"I am Greek," I said. "Are there other Greeks there?"

"Many, and they're all gathered together. Besides, all nationalities can be found there. We are free. We visit each other."

"We're going too," I said to Giuseppe. "There's no other way. We have to find a place to settle. I suggest we go up and have a look. They separate nationalities, but we can still get together."

After taking the number of the tram and all other information from the Italians, we rushed to meet our friends. First we gave them bread, which was all we managed to have, and then told them the news.

"We're thinking about our going up to that camp. Each of us will be obliged to join the group of his country," I said, "but I think this is best for us. We will still be together and able to see each other anytime. What do you say? Do you agree?"

They agreed unanimously. So we boarded the little tram where we found other Italians and after a twenty-minute ride, got off at the correct stop. We had arrived on a high hill able to see the whole of Berlin below.

Entering the camp gate, they asked whether we were newcomers.

"Yes," we answered.

"Then, separate into nationalities, give us some identification, and we shall guide you in. The three girls will go down below to the right to join the Greeks.

Come with us, we'll get you settled," somebody said to us. "Take a laissez-passer from here which you will need to go in and out, and show each time at the gate. The Italians stay exactly opposite the Greeks. Here everybody is free and you can go wherever you wish. Yugoslavians, please come this way to join your countrymen."

And so, our small group parted there with great emotion and relief. Each of us went to meet our countrymen with whom we would later be repatriated.

Our Greek group

At the Greek area there were a number of small houses, like small flats. When we arrived many Greek men and women were

A Cry for Tomorrow 76859 ...

outside, who, in the beginning looked at us oddly. Most were busy with their housework and cooking. We introduced ourselves and told them we were three Jewish girls from Greece who survived the crematoria, and came now to join them to go back to Greece together. They stood with their mouths wide open, never having heard anything like it. In all there were about eighty poor Greek workers, all Christian Orthodox, who had come to Germany to work. The war broke out and after much suffering, they were liberated at the end by the Russians. They asked to be repatriated to see their homes again.

We learned the Russians distributed food, oil, and butter. The people had frying pans, utensils and were cooking whatever they liked. Those who smoked were even given tobacco.

Listening to our story of the crematoria these people were very moved and showed much understanding. Then our guides prepared three nice beds with sheets and blankets and settled us immediately.

One by one others came to meet us, to introduce themselves, and to show support and offer assistance. All readily helped us, as best they could. They recommended that for the first few days we should not be concerned by anything apart from ourselves. To just eat, drink, and rest. Apparently we were very thin and looking awful, so that is what we did. After two or three days they were calling us their "little sisters." Even now, remembering them, I am full of emotion. At the time, they were real angels whom God had finally sent our way!

This place on the hill was in a very beautiful setting. Trees lined the back, and one could see an immense forest stretching far into the distance. It was a perfect place to recuperate. Right away everyone pitched in to erect swings with ropes attached to the trees so their little sisters, Berry, Paula, and Frieda could swing and enjoy themselves.

"We must help these poor girls recover quickly and get them back to their homes as soon as possible. And listen carefully," they added, "if you don't find any of your family in Greece, don't be afraid. Come to our homes." After the enormous psychological stress suffered during the war, those poor sweet Greeks had rich feelings and generously expressed how they felt.

It was like a holiday for us. We miserable Auschwitz survivors began recovering physically at least, for we were sleeping well and eating sufficiently. The Russians gave us the same portions as everyone else. For recreation, we were swinging on the swings, sometimes taking short walks to the edge of the forest, and once in a while, even went down to Berlin by tram.

Indeed, after a short period we were feeling entirely different, and as if by a miracle, Paula's legs improved and she hardly suffered anymore. She could run and jump like a rabbit. From then on, we understood we had become human beings again as we used to be.

We frequently met with our previous group of Yugoslavians and Italians even though each of us gradually gravitated to those of our own nationality. Giuseppe remained an integral member of our company though, and we continued to go out every afternoon. We walked around the grounds, the forest, or went down to Berlin.

Our Greek group was well accepted, and generally people of different ethnic background communicated well with each other and had good relations. We stayed in that place for almost a month and a half, long enough to start feeling homesick for our country.

Fortunately, our group was well organized, had established connections with Greeks from other camps, and knew what was going on all over Greece and Germany. It continuously and insistently sought a quicker way of being repatriated than that promised by the Russians.

From time to time, this group informed active members — those whom they trusted — of their activities. Among those few were the three of us Jewish girls. I appreciated that my opinion was very important to them and that before making any move, they asked for my advice. Of the things we discussed, nothing ever leaked out. Everything was kept confidential and secret. In this way, I belonged to a Greek organization outside the homeland that was very interesting and exciting.

Decampment of the Greeks

Immediately after the end of World War II, Berlin was divided between the four great powers: The Americans, the Russians, the French, and the British.

One day our Greek friends came as always to tell us the news: "Girls, everything is ready! We leave tomorrow at 2:00 a.m. — all eighty Greeks — for the American sector. We learned the Americans are sending all foreigners like us back much more quickly. Airplanes are being used for repatriation. We will leave here through the middle of the forest, not by the central gate, so the Russians won't notice our moves before all of us are gone."

I remember I saw Giuseppe that afternoon as always, and said "good-night" to him without a hint about our plan. Nobody knew anything apart from us Greeks.

That night not one of us slept. Ready and dressed, all eighty of us

A Cry for Tomorrow 76859 ...

gathered whatever personal or necessary things we had and very carefully left by the backside of the forest. It was pitch dark everywhere.... We tiptoed, silently like cats so as not to be heard. Two or three guides, who rode 100 to 200 meters ahead on their bikes, returned to tell us that our road was free. So very slowly and with great caution, we crossed the forest and found ourselves all together down in East Berlin where we finally boarded the subway.

Gathered one next to the other, we followed our guides who held maps they had studied. I remember we changed three or four underground lines and destinations, sometimes at a lower level, sometimes at a higher one, until about twelve o'clock noon we reached the camp which was supervised by the Americans. There, American soldiers received us very politely, took down our identity information, and immediately provided us with food and shelter.

Our Greek guides came to say good-bye. They were happy and pleased that everything worked out and that everybody had reached the American side. Eighty Greeks, safe and sound!

"Dear friends," I said, "won't you stay with us?"

"No, we're going back there again, we have more work to do, but we'll be back."

"Could you do me a favor?"

"Whatever you wish."

"Well, since you are going back where we were, I'll give you a little letter to take to the side where the Italians stay. Ask for Giuseppe Lucarelli please, and give it to him personally. Is this possible?"

"Yes, of course it is. Write it quickly, we'll take it and leave."

I immediately took a piece of paper and a pencil, and quickly wrote in Italian the following:

Dear Giuseppe,

After you read my note, if you yourself really want to, please follow this young Greek with confidence. He will explain, and bring you here where we all are.

Love,
Berry

Two days later I couldn't believe my eyes! I thought I was dreaming. In disbelief, I saw Giuseppe again coming toward us, escorted by our young Greek guide.

Giuseppe greeted us joyfully. "I was mad with joy when I read the note you sent me," he said smiling. "I really didn't want to believe that we parted in such an awful way without your saying good-bye to me. Everyone back there is still confused. They can't believe how all the Greeks, without exception, disappeared so suddenly. Of course, I said nothing to anybody. I trusted you so much that I followed the young Greek without any discussion or hesitation."

Here there were other Italians, so after giving identification information, Giuseppe settled in with his co-patriots. As before in the other camp, we now saw each other as usual.

After a few days, the Americans moved all of us to a nice place near the railway lines. As time went on the Italians were increasing daily, so much so that finally they were like a large battalion. All were former prisoners of war and had to be repatriated as soon as possible. Indeed, the Italians would be sent home to Italy by train in the next twenty or thirty days, they said.

When the day of departure for the Italians finally arrived, Giuseppe was agitated and very nervous. He confessed that he didn't want to leave without me, and with great emotion, proposed I go with him to Italy and marry him. He also explained to me that his parents were strict Catholics and very religious.

Despite the fact that I was very moved by his proposal, I realized deep inside I was not yet ready to face either marriage or, above all, a change in my religion. I still felt wounded by the injustice done to me ... charging me only with being a Jew. From the time I was taken to the concentration camp, the subject of my religion was very painful for me and touching upon it now was very premature.

Just then, at the moment of my embarrassment of having to answer Giuseppe, an Italian officer and leader of his fellow countrymen, like *deus ex machina,* intervened and said to him: "No, no foreign woman can possibly come with us to Italy." (Perhaps Paula also played a role, as she felt she would die of sorrow if I left her side. At least this is what I suspect.)

Giuseppe was a wonderful man of great dignity. I met him at a difficult time immediately after my liberation, and he was very supportive of me and of all the others. I didn't want to hurt him, but I felt very relieved that I couldn't possibly go with him or have to explain all the things I was thinking. We exchanged addresses and decided to first go to our homelands and then write each other.

The following day, Paula, Frieda, and I went down to the railway station to say good-bye to Giuseppe who was finally leaving for Italy. Our separation was very emotional! The last image of him, which I still see before me, was his hand waving to me from the train's window as it was moving away with great speed, until it suddenly disappeared.

I stayed for some time, standing there thoughtfully. "What will you do, Berry, now that Giuseppe is gone?" And I remember, as if it were yesterday, how I replied to myself: "It ends here. You must forget him forever and never write to him. Let him take his own road with his own people. And you Berry, take yours — where you belong."

Brussels

A few days later, if I remember well, they put us in some decent buses and drove first to Munich. After a two-day stay, we were taken again by bus to Brussels. There we entered an immense place where the Americans were accommodating prisoners from all over Europe. It was to be our last stop before repatriation by airplane. They said we had to register quickly for a priority number that would enable us to leave for Greece a few at a time.

In the meantime, until our turn came up, the Americans cared for us kindly. We ate and drank lavishly as much as we wanted, as if we were in the best restaurants of Europe. Even medical care was provided. I remember that my friend Erica, whom I met there, came down with acute appendicitis. The best doctors operated on her immediately, and she soon recovered.

Apart from Erica, I found many girlfriends, former Auschwitz prisoners, with whom I worked in *Kanada*. From them I learned with great sorrow that Alegra Kamhi had been killed on a motorcycle in Noestad, just one month after her liberation. On the other hand, Erica found her brother Raoul, and was brimming with joy.

During the period of our stay with the Americans, lots of people arrived. I met fellow Kastorians whom I hadn't seen since Birkenau at Block 27. We sought information from each other about those who were not among us, and so many were missing. Nobody had seen any of my relatives, or any of my family.

Apart from the flow of people inside, almost every day we had visitors from the city. They came asking about their own surviving relatives. One day two Kastorian Christian couples came who had been living in Brussels for years as furriers. They made a great impression on me. They asked about their co-patriots, the Jews of Kastoria.

"I am from Kastoria," I said, "and so are these four or five girls next to me."

"Who are you?" we asked.

They replied they were of the Yata family from Kastoria. Then I related how I knew their parents and their other brothers who were my close neighbors in Kastoria. Immediately, with great affection, they invited us to their homes and showed sincere interest in helping us.

We developed very close ties with these friends and frequently went to visit them as if they were truly our relatives. Above all, their two very sweet wives, who originally came from a Greek island, looked after us in unimaginable ways. They received us with kindness for which we were very grateful. Besides, these were the first substantial homes we saw after the war and our internment.

One day, the Americans distributed a generous sum of money to each one of us, so we could circulate comfortably in and around the city. I was given money also, and as I was standing on the tram in Brussels, someone apparently put his hand in my pocket and stole it all. When I realized it, I immediately told Paula who got very upset. "God, what are you going to do now?" she said.

Her question sounded so ridiculous to me, it started me laughing. "Whatever I did all this time since my liberation," I replied. "Did I have money yesterday or the day before yesterday? Don't worry, money will come back again. After everything we've been through, haven't you learned yet what life is all about?"

I don't know how I arranged it, but the following day we all went as a large group on a bus excursion to Waterloo. I liked the entire place very much. The guided tour was excellent, for they explained how right here at Waterloo, Napoleon the Great lost his last battle after so very many victories.

"Mr. Napoleon," I said to him. "Whoever has thirst for war and wants to conquer the world by killing, will one day himself fall in a last battle called 'Waterloo'."

A marriage proposal

One day the two Yata couples (the husbands were brothers) proposed that I marry a Jewish friend of theirs, a good man, they said, who wanted to get married to a girl who returned from the Holocaust.

"Because we are so very fond of you, Berry, and are our compatriot, we urged him to marry you. What do you say?"

"It is very kind of you to do this, and I appreciate it very much. I thank you particularly for your interest in me. But I must not, I think, get married yet. I believe my first priority is to go back home to Greece a free woman."

A Cry for Tomorrow 76859 ...

Paula cried for joy when she heard my final decision. "Bravo, Berry dear, don't leave me in the middle of the road.... You promised you would take me all the way to Greece. You shouldn't marry here."

"But Paula dear," I responded laughing, "you don't need me anymore. You're just fine. Apart from me there are now other people we know, and I'm sure you can manage by yourself!"

"Only you count for me," she said.

Adoption proposal

One day, a wealthy Jewish couple named Rikanati, both somewhat up in years, came to the place where we were staying. They decided to adopt a girl from a camp of the Holocaust because they had no children. Having come and gone for many days, they came straight to me after becoming interested and taking a great liking to me. They had even sought information and knew I originated from Kastoria, etc.

Lo and behold, now both came smiling, happy to make me a very beautiful, kind proposal: that they very much desired to adopt me as their child. They promised me the moon and the stars. Whatever I wished for would be at my disposal, especially studies and anything else. This proposal seemed unreal to me. How could I, I wondered, acquire parents again at my age?

It was very difficult for me to tell them I couldn't do it at this time because I didn't want to sadden and disappoint them. I kept thanking them for their partiality, but said I very much wanted to go first to Greece to verify with my own eyes, who of my family survived. After that, I would make my decision. I promised I would write as soon as I arrived in Greece.

The one who benefited every time I said "no" was Paula. She selfishly wanted me at her side until Greece. One other day, I recall, I had the opportunity to fly round trip from Brussels to Paris for a week. Paula started crying like a baby and was unyielding. She just wouldn't let me go. And so I didn't.

Repatriation

Military planes full of former prisoners kept leaving for various countries. Finally our turn came. They announced we would be departing for Greece by air!

I was very upset that day because this time I was returning completely alone, without anyone from my family. I didn't know what to expect, or whom I would find there. At the airport, just before boarding the plane, I turned my head for a few moments to look far into the distance at the horizon. I returned to all those countries and cities I was leaving behind. How many hardships I had endured on the way here! Sometimes by train, sometimes on foot, by truck, by bus, and now by American military plane.

Feeling dizzy, I went in, and as there were no seats, we were all huddled together waiting for the endless hours of travel in the air to pass before reaching our final destination — Athens.

After we took off, I had no appetite to talk to anyone. I told Paula, who was next to me, that I wanted to sleep. I closed my eyes and sank into my thoughts and recollections. I remembered the recent experiences of the camp, the crematoria of Auschwitz-Birkenau. I saw again that endless Death March, then Ravensbruck, Retsov, Malhov. All that suffering, each of which alone caused me so much pain.

I brought to mind everything that had happened to me in my life, and as I visualized all those many images, my feelings became confused. But soon, I felt something warm and alive well up inside me, and I wondered what it was. Then I knew that it was life itself inside me, warm and luminous, as it moves from birth to death.

I looked intensely at my hands, those thin, sensitive hands that I almost lost. I then touched my hair, my eyes, my ears, my face, my arms, my neck, my legs ... then my belly, saved from Dr. Mengele's scalpel — from the experiments. I was flooded by a strange feeling that my body was now a "miracle"! A miracle that emerged living and whole and was not burned in the crematoria of Auschwitz.

This body which survived, had a soul within it, however, that suffered much, that underwent great misfortune, disappointment, injustice, pain, betrayal, disease, crimes; but at the same time acquired enormous strength, and learned the meaning of devotion, love, and compassion. All this was very significant. I thought that no one could understand these things if they had not lived through them themselves, as I did so intensely. For I, I was very rich in struggle and very rich in pain, but I was very rich in soul.

Postscript

Below are a few notes about the author and the fate or whereabouts of her family and friends who appear in the book. This section was not a part of the original Greek publication.

Berry Nahmia
Today, Berry Nahmia is the happy mother of two children, grandmother to two grandchildren, and great-grandmother to four great-grandchildren.... After publishing her book, *A Cry For Tomorrow*, she became president of the "Greek Survivors of the Holocaust Organization" and works tirelessly toward honoring the memory of the millions unjustly lost. She lectures in schools and participates in international conferences. She has organized the video-taping of survivors' accounts in order that their testimonies of the Holocaust remain as a living historical record without falsification.

For her work with survivors, she has studied philosophy and Adlerian psychology and in all of her activities, it is clearly evident, that she loves human beings without regard to ethnic origin, or religion, and that she abhors intolerance and racism.

Allegra Korman
My cousin Gita, whose real name is Allegra, survived and soon after returning to Greece left for America. There she married an American Jew, Leonard Korman, and has two children and four grandchildren. She lives in Los Angeles, California.

We continue to have a very close relationship and see each other often. Sometimes she comes to Greece or I visit her in America, especially for a family Bar Mitzvah or wedding. During those visits we reminisce about our childhood, our parents, our relatives, and friends.

Gita has also written her memories in English as a legacy to her children and future generations.

Dora Russo
My friend Dora survived. She lives in Israel on the Moshav, Kfar-Sirkin — a modern village of Petah Tikva.

After her liberation, she returned to her native Yugoslavia where she married Dario Russo, a fine husband very much admired and respected by my own husband and myself. She has two children, a boy and a girl.

After repatriation, we lost contact with each other for a period of three years. Then one day, quite by chance, I learned from a friend who knew us both, that Dora was living in Israel. I travelled there immediately to find her and since then we have kept in constant touch. We continue to have a deep personal relationship. She is still one of the few people in the world to whom I am able to speak about what is most dear to my heart, because her philosophy and the manner in which she thinks so enraptures me. She still has the power to impart to me strength and the desire to live.

We often speak of our lives in the camp and I learn new details of the clever, incredible things she did there, especially to survive. But now she likes to tell me how she admires the fact that it is I who has become the strong and capable one.

Dora lives alone now because her wonderful companion, her husband, passed away. Nevertheless, she has many friends and neighbors who love and feel compassion for her.

Other Victims and Survivors

My brother Alberto, three years younger than I, never entered the work force of the camp because he was taken immediately to the crematory. From that moment, I never saw him again and for a long time, my memory of him was always accompanied by guilt. I don't know why, but I kept asking myself why he wasn't next to me, why he wasn't saved. After all, he was so young.

How I regret that I never found even one photograph of him. His image, though, is very clearly engraved in my mind, and when I close my eyes I always find him ... just as he was then, a young innocent lad.

My half brothers and sisters from my stepmother, who were all under ten years of age; my dear father Israel; my grandmother Boena; my grandfather Jacob; and my many not-to-be-forgotten aunts and uncles — all were devoured by the flames of the crematoria.

Of my six inseparable friends, only three survived: Lena Eliaou, Stella Eliaou, and myself, Berry Kassoutou. Rebecca Zacharia, Rebecca Pissirilou, and Paula Cohen never returned.

My friend Lena married in America the Kastorian Moise Russo, a Holocaust survivor. They have three boys and five grandchildren. Stella also married a Kastorian survivor, Pepo Cohen, and they have

POSTSCRIPT

two sons and many grandchildren in Israel.

Of the approximately 1,000 Jewish inhabitants of Kastoria, only thirty-two survived the camps and returned. Another three survived by hiding in the mountains of Greece. A total of thirty-five!

Glossary

Appell Roll call of concentration camp prisoners

Blockoberst Block warden

"Final Solution" Nazi term for the extermination of the Jews

Hauptsturmbannführer Captain

Kanada The complex in Birkenau where the belongings of newly arrived prisoners were sorted and stored. The name "Canada" symbolized a place of wealth and riches.

Kanadakommando The name of the work unit(s) who worked in Kanada

Kapo(s) Concentration camp prisoner(s) placed in charge of inmate laborers

Kommando Labor or work detail

Lumpensammlerin Woman rag collector

Oberscharführer SS technical sergeant

Politische Abteilung An organization of the Gestapo that spied on prisoners, civilian employees, and SS alike. They investigated escapes and conspiracies.

Selektion Euphemism for the process of choosing victims for the gas chamber or forced labor

Sonderkommando "Special squad". The Jewish units in extermination camps who removed the bodies of those gassed for cremation or burial.

SS Schutzstaffel, meaning "Protection Squad." Elite units of the Nazi Party under Himmler

Staplerin Stacker

Stubenoberst Leader of the room or hall

Stuka German war plane

Unterscharführer SS sergeant

Verflucht Cursed

Vorarbeiter A prisoner foreman

Zlotys A monetary unit (coin) of Poland

Appendix

A Cry for Tomorrow 76859 ...

Page from Auschwitz records indi

APPENDIX

tattoo number for Berry Cassuto

A Cry for Tomorrow 76859 ...

Oswiecim-Brzezinka, July 16th, 1987

L. dz.

IV-8521/2476/2090/87

The State Oswiecim-Brzezinka Museum

          Mrs. Bonica Cassuto-Nahmias
          13 Cokkinaki St.
          KIFISSIA – ATHENS
          Greece

The State Oswiecim-Brzezinka Museum confirms that Bonica CASSUTO, age 20, arrived in the concentration camp in Oswiecim / KL Auschwitz-Birkenau / on April 11th, 1944, in RSHA transport from Athens / Castoria/. Her inmate number was 76859.

No further information is available.

The source of information: KL Auschwitz-Birkenau transportation lists and medical documentation by SS Doctor, Josef Mengele, M.D.

                        Director

                        / mgr Kazimierz Smolen /

Attachment:
Xerox copy of a document.

Appendix

Oświęcim - Brzezinka, dn 16 lipca 1987 r.

L. dz. IV-6521/2476/2090 /87/

PAŃSTWOWE MUZEUM OŚWIĘCIM BRZEZINKA

NBP OŚWIĘCIM
KONTO 718-92-7

CENTRALA TELEF.
20-21 – 20-24

MUZEUM CZYNNE
CODZIENNIE
W GODZ. 8-15
OPRÓCZ
PONIEDZIAŁKÓW
I DNI
POŚWIĄTECZNYCH

PRZYJAZD
ZWIEDZAJĄCYCH
NALEŻY
WCZEŚNIEJ
ZGŁOSIĆ

Pani Bonica C a s s u t o – Nahmias
13 Cokkinaki St.
K I F I S S I A – ATHENS

Grecja

Państwowe Muzeum w Oświęcimiu zaświadcza, że
C A S S U T O Bonica lat 20, została przywieziona
do obozu koncentracyjnego w Oświęcimiu /KL Auschwitz-
Birkenau/ w dniu 11.4.1944 r. transportem RSHA z Aten
/Castoria/. ---------------------------------
w obozie oznaczona numerem 76859. -------------------
Innych danych o wyżej wymienionej Muzeum nie posiada.

PODSTAWA informacji:
--------------------- numerowe wykazy transportów
przybyłych do obozu koncentracyjnego
w Oświęcimiu /KL Auschwitz-Birkenau/ oraz
dokumenty dotyczące pomiarów antropologicznych
wykonanych na więźniach, na polecenie SS-mana
dr Mengele. -----------------------------

D Y R E K T O R
/mgr Kazimierz Smoleń/

Załącznik:
kserokopia dokumentu

ZGPT Oświęcim, zam. 210 t. IV. 75 50.000

[The Seal: State Museum, 32-603 Oswiecim]

KL Auschwitz

The anthropometric measurements made due to the orders of SS-Doctor, Josef Mengele, M.D.

The entry concerns Bonica CASSUTO, age 20, the inmate no. 76859.

July 10th, 1987

APPENDIX

> KL Auschwitz
> Pomiary antropologiczne wykonane na polecenie
> SS-mana dr Mengele w obozie KL Auschwitz
> Wpis ołówcy więzniarki Nr 76859
> CASSUTO Bonice lot 20

PAŃSTWOWE MUZEUM
32-603 Oświęcim 5
10/7.87

www.ingramcontent.com/pod-product-compliance
Lightning Source LLC
Chambersburg PA
CBHW050758160426
43192CB00010B/1556